2nd Workshop on South and Southeast Asian Natural Language Processing 2011

(WSSANLP 2011)

Held at the 5th International Joint Conference on Natural Language Processing 2011 (IJCNLP 2011)

Chiang Mai, Thailand
8 November 2011

ISBN: 978-1-62276-441-9

Printed from e-media with permission by:

Curran Associates, Inc.
57 Morehouse Lane
Red Hook, NY 12571

Some format issues inherent in the e-media version may also appear in this print version.

Printed by Curran Associates, Inc. (2012)

For permission requests, please contact the Association for Computational Linguistics at the address below.

Association for Computational Linguistics
209 N. Eighth Street
Stroudsburg, Pennsylvania 18360

Phone: 1-570-476-8006
Fax: 1-570-476-0860

acl@aclweb.org

Additional copies of this publication are available from:

Curran Associates, Inc.
57 Morehouse Lane
Red Hook, NY 12571 USA
Phone: 845-758-0400
Fax: 845-758-2634
Email: curran@proceedings.com
Web: www.proceedings.com

Table of Contents

Preface

Welcome to the IJCNLP Workshop on South and Southeast Asian Natural Language Processing (WSSANLP). South Asia comprises of the countries, Afghanistan, Bangladesh, Bhutan, India, Maldives, Nepal, Pakistan and Sri Lanka. Southeast Asia, on the other hand, consists of Brunei, Burma, Cambodia, East Timor, Indonesia, Laos, Malaysia, Philippines, Singapore, Thailand and Vietnam.

This area is the home to thousands of languages that belong to different language families like Indo-Aryan, Indo-Iranian, Dravidian, Sino-Tibetan, Austro-Asiatic, Kradai, Hmong-Mien, etc. In terms of population, South Asian and Southeast Asia represent 35 percent of the total population of the world which means as much as 2.5 billion speakers. Some of the languages of these regions have a large number of native speakers: Hindi (5th largest according to number of its native speakers), Bengali (6th), Punjabi (12th), Tamil(18th), Urdu (20th), etc.

As internet and electronic devices including PCs and hand held devices including mobile phones have spread far and wide in the region, it has become imperative to develop language technology for these languages. It is important for economic development as well as for social and individual progress.

A characteristic of these languages is that they are under-resourced. The words of these languages show rich variations in morphology. Moreover they are often heavily agglutinated and synthetic, making segmentation an important issue. The intellectual motivation for this workshop comes from the need to explore ways of harnessing the morphology of these languages for higher level processing. The task of morphology, however, in South and Southeast Asian Languages is intimately linked with segmentation for these languages.

The goal of WSSANLP is:

• Providing a platform to linguistic and NLP communities for sharing and discussing ideas and work on South and Southeast Asian languages and combining efforts.
• Development of useful and high quality computational resources for under resourced South and Southeast Asian languages.

We are delighted to present to you this volume of proceedings of 2nd Workshop on South and Southeast Asian NLP. We have received 15 long and short submissions. On the basis of our review process, we have competitively selected 9 papers.

We look forward to an invigorating workshop.

Rajeev Sangal (Chair WSSANLP),
IIIT Hyderabad, India

M.G. Abbas Malik (Chair of Organizing Committee WSSANLP),
Faculty of Computing and Information Technology (North Branch),
King Abdulaziz University, Saudi Arabia

2nd Workshop on South and Southeast Asian Natural Language processing

Workshop Chair:

Rajeev Sangal, IIIT Hyderabad, India

Workshop Organization Co-chair:

M. G. Abbas Malik, Faculty of Computing and Information Technology (North Branch), King Abdulaziz University, Saudi Arabia

Invited Speaker:

Pushpak Bhattacharyya, IIT Bombay, India

Organizers:

Aasim Ali, Punjab University College of Information Technology, University of the Punjab, Pakistan
Amitava Das, Jadavpur Univeristy, India
Fahad Iqbal Khan, COMSATS IIT Lahore, Pakistan
M. G. Abbas Malik, King Abdulaziz University, Saudi Arabia
Smriti Singh, Indian Institute of Technology Bombay (IITB), India

Program Committee:

Sivaji Bandyopadhyay, Jadavpur University, India
Vincent Berment, GETALP-LIG / INALCO, France
Laurent Besacier, GETALP-LIG, Université de Grenoble, France
Pushpak Bhattacharyya, IIT Bombay, India
Hervé Blanchon, GETALP-LIG, Université de Grenoble, France
Christian Boitet, GETALP-LIG, Université de Grenoble, France
Miriam Butt, University of Konstanz, Germany
Nicola Cancedda, Xerox Research Center Europe (XRCE), France
Eric Castelli, International Research Center MICA, Vietnam
Laurence Danlos, University of Paris 7, France
Georges Fafiotte, GETALP-LIG, Université de Grenoble, France
Zulfiqar HabibCOMSATS Institute of Information Technology, Pakistan
Sarmad Hussain, Al-Khawarizmi Institute of Computer Science, University of Engineering and Technology, Pakistan
Aravind K. Joshi, University of Pennsylvania, USA
Abid Khan, University of Peshawar, Pakistan
Krit KOSAWAT, Human Language Technology Laboratory (HLT) National Electronics and Computer Technology Center (NECTEC), Thailand
Bal Krishna Bal, University of Kathmandu, Nepal
A. Kumaran, Microsoft Research, India
Gurpreet Singh Lehal, Punjabi University Patiala, India
Haizhou Li, Institute for Infocomm Research, Singapore
M. G. Abbas Malik, King Abdulaziz University, Saudi Arabia
Bali Ranaivo-Malançon, Multimedia University, Malaysia

Hammam Riza, Agency for the Assessment and Application of Technology (BPPT), Indonesia
Rajeev Sangal, IIIT Hyderabad, India
L. Sobha, AU-KBC Research Centre, Chennai, India
Ruvan Weerasinghe, University of Colombo School of Computing, Sri Lanka

We wish to thank our sponsors

Gold Sponsors

www.google.com

www.baidu.com

The Office of Naval Research (ONR)

The Asian Office of Aerospace Research and Development (AOARD)

Department of Systems Engineering and Engineering Managment, The Chinese University of Hong Kong

Silver Sponsors

Microsoft Corporation

Bronze Sponsors

Chinese and Oriental Languages Information Processing Society (COLIPS)

Supporter

Thailand Convention and Exhibition Bureau (TCEB)

We wish to thank our sponsors

Organizers

Asian Federation of Natural Language Processing (AFNLP)

National Electronics and Computer Technology Center (NECTEC), Thailand

Sirindhorn International Institute of Technology (SIIT), Thailand

Rajamangala University of Technology Lanna (RMUTL), Thailand

Maejo University, Thailand

Chiang Mai University (CMU), Thailand

Program the 2nd Workshop on South and Southeast Asian Natural Language Processing

Tuesday, November 8, 2011

8:30–8:45 Opening Remarks

8:45–10:00 Invited Talk by Pushpak Bhattacharyya

10:00–10:30 Break

WSSANLP Session I

10:30–11:00 *Hybrid Inflectional Stemmer and Rule-based Derivational Stemmer for Gujarati*
Kartik Suba, Dipti Jiandani and Pushpak Bhattacharyya

11:00–11:30 *Improving Persian-English Statistical Machine Translation:Experiments in Domain Adaptation*
Mahsa Mohaghegh, Abdolhossein Sarrafzadeh and Tom Moir

11:30–12:00 *Thai Word Segmentation Verification Tool*
Supon Klaithin, Kanyanut Kriengket, Sitthaa Phaholphinyo and Krit Kosawat

12:00–12:30 *The Semi-Automatic Construction of Part-Of-Speech Taggers for Specific Languages by Statistical Methods*
Tomohiro YAMASAKI, Hiromi WAKAKI and Masaru SUZUKI

12:30–14:00 Lunch Break

WSSANLP Session II

14:00–14:30 *Towards a Malay Derivational Lexicon: Learning Affixes Using Expectation Maximization*
Suriani Sulaiman, Michael Gasser and Sandra Kuebler

14:30–15:00 *Punjabi Language Stemmer for nouns and proper names*
Vishal Gupta and Gurpreet Singh Lehal

15:00–15:30 *Challenges in Urdu Text Tokenization and Sentence Boundary Disambiguation*
Zobia Rehman, Waqas Anwar and Usama Ijaz Bajwa

15:30–16:00 Break

Tuesday, November 8, 2011 (continued)

WSSANLP Session III

16:00–16:30	*Challenges in Developing a Rule based Urdu Stemmer* Sajjad Ahmad Khan, Waqas Anwar and Usama Ijaz Bajwa
16:30–17:00	*Developing a New System for Arabic Morphological Analysis and Generation* Mourad Gridach and Noureddine Chenfour
17:00–17:15	Closing Remarks

Hybrid Inflectional Stemmer and Rule-based Derivational Stemmer for Gujarati

Kartik Suba **Dipti Jiandani**
Department of Computer Engineering
Dharmsinh Desai University
suba.kartik@gmail.com
jiandani.dipti@gmail.com

Pushpak Bhattacharyya
Department of Computer Science and Engineering
Indian Institute of Technology Bombay
pb@cse.iitb.ac.in

Abstract

In this paper we present two stemmers for Gujarati- a lightweight inflectional stemmer based on a hybrid approach and a heavyweight derivational stemmer based on a rule-based approach. Besides using a module for unsupervised learning of stems and suffixes for lightweight stemming, we have also included a module performing POS (Part Of Speech) based stemming and a module using a set of substitution rules, in order to improve the quality of these stems and suffixes. The inclusion of these modules boosted the accuracy of the inflectional stemmer by 9.6% and 12.7% respectively, helping us achieve an accuracy of 90.7%. The maximum index compression obtained for the inflectional stemmer is about 95%. On the other hand, the derivational stemmer is completely rule-based, for which, we attained an accuracy of 70.7% with the help of suffix-stripping, substitution and orthographic rules. Both these systems were developed to be useful in applications such as Information Retrieval, corpus compression, dictionary search and as pre-processing modules in other NLP problems such as WSD.

1. Introduction

Stemming is a process of conflating related words to a common stem by chopping off the inflectional and derivational endings.

Stemming plays a vital role in Information Retrieval systems by reducing the index size and increasing the recall by retrieving results that contain any of the possible forms of a word present in the query (Harman, 1991). This is especially true in case of a morphologically rich language like Gujarati.

The aim is to ensure that all the related words map to common stem, wherein, the stem may or may not be a meaningful word in the vocabulary of the language.

Current state of the art approaches to stemming can be classified into three categories, viz., rule-based, unsupervised and hybrid (Smirnov, 2008). In case of inflectional stemmer, building a completely rule-based system is non-trivial for a language like Gujarati. On the other hand, adopting a purely unsupervised approach, such as *take-all-splits* discussed in section 4, may fail to take advantage of some language phenomena, such as, the suffixes in a language like Gujarati, are separable based on their parts of speech. For example, the suffix ી (*-ī*) should be stripped off for verbs (as in case of કરી *karī* 'did'), but not for nouns (as in case of ઈમાનદારી *īmāndārī* 'honesty'). Such characteristics can be easily represented in the form of substitution rules. So, we follow a hybrid approach for the inflectional stemmer taking advantage of both rule-based and unsupervised phenomena.

However, in case of derivational stemming, words that are derived, either by adding affixes to the stems or by performing changes at the morpheme boundary, are reduced to their stem forms. To accomplish this task of derivational stemming, we have adopted a completely rule-based approach.

The remainder of this paper is organized as follows. We describe the related work in section 2. Next, section 3 explains the morphological structure of Gujarati. We describe our approach to inflectional stemmer in section 4 and to derivational stemmer in section 5. Experiments and results are presented in section 6. Section 7 concludes the paper, pointing also to future work.

Proceedings of the 2nd Workshop on South and Southeast Asian Natural Language Processing (WSSANLP), IJCNLP 2011, , pages 1–8,
Chiang Mai, Thailand, November 8, 2011.

2. Background and Related Work

The earliest English stemmer was developed by Julie Beth Lovins (1968). The Porter stemming algorithm (Martin Porter, 1980), which was published later, is perhaps the most widely used algorithm for stemming in case of English language. Both of these stemmers are rule-based and are best suited for less inflectional languages like English.

A lot of work has been done in the field of unsupervised learning of morphology. Goldsmith (2001) proposed an unsupervised approach for learning the morphology of a language based on the Minimum Description Length (MDL) framework which focuses on representing the data in as compact manner as possible.

Not much work has been reported for stemming for Indian languages compared to English and other European languages. The earliest work reported by Ramanathan and Rao (2003) used a hand crafted suffix list and performed longest match stripping for building a Hindi stemmer. Majumder et al. (2007) developed YASS: Yet Another Suffix Stripper which uses a clustering-based approach based on string distance measures and requires no linguistic knowledge. Pandey and Siddiqui (2008) proposed an unsupervised stemming algorithm for Hindi based on Goldsmith's (2001) approach.

Work has also been done for Gujarati. Inspired by Goldsmith (2001), a lightweight statistical stemmer was built for Gujarati (Patel et al., 2010) which gave an accuracy of 68%. But no work was done so far in the area of derivational stemming for Gujarati.

3. Gujarati Morphology

The Gujarati phoneme set consists of eight vowels and twenty-four consonants. Gujarati is rich in its morphology, which means, grammatical information is encoded by the way of affixation rather than independent free-standing morphemes.

The Gujarati nouns inflect for number (singular, plural), gender (masculine, feminine, neuter), and declension class (absolute, oblique). The absolute form of a noun is its default or uninflected form. This form is used as the object of the verb, typically when inanimate as well as in measure or temporal construction. There are seven oblique forms in Gujarati corresponding more or less to the case forms- nominative, dative, instrumental, ablative, genitive, locative and vocative. All cases, except for the vocative, are distinguished by means of postpositions.

The Gujarati adjectives are of two types – declinable and indeclinable. The declinable adjectives have the termination *-ũ* (ુ ં) in neuter absolute. The masculine absolute of these adjectives ends in *-o* (ો) and the feminine absolute in *-ī* (ી). For example, the adjective સારું *sārũ* 'good' takes the form સારું *sārũ*, સારો *sāro* and સારી *sārī* when used for a neuter, masculine and feminine object respectively. These adjectives agree with the noun they qualify in gender, number and case. Adjectives that do not end in *-ũ* in neuter absolute singular are classified as indeclinable and remain unaltered when affixed to a noun.

The Gujarati verbs are inflected based on a combination of gender, number, person, aspect, tense and mood. There are several postpositions in Gujarati which get bound to the nouns or verbs which they postposition. For example, *-nũ* (નું : genitive marker), *-mā̃* (માં : in), *-e* (ે : ergative marker), etc. These postpositions get agglutinated to nouns or verbs and do not merely follow them. For example, the phrase 'in water' is expressed in Gujarati as a single word પાણીમાં *pāṇīmā̃*, wherein, માં *mā̃* is agglutinated to the noun પાણી *pāṇī*.

We created four lists of Gujarati suffixes which contain postpositions and inflectional suffixes respectively for nouns, verbs, adjectives and adverbs for use in our approach for the inflectional stemmer. Similar lists have been used for the derivational stemmer, in the form of orthographic, suffix-stripping and substitution rules.

4. Our Approach for Inflectional Stemmer

We have been inspired by Goldsmith (2001). Goldsmith's approach was based on unsupervised learning of stems and suffixes, and he proposed a *take-all-splits* method. Besides this, we have incorporated two more modules, one performing POS-based stemming and the other doing suffix-stripping based on linguistic rules. During the training phase of our approach, the Gujarati words extracted from EMILLE corpus[1] are used in order to learn the probable stems and suffixes. This information is used in order to stem any unseen data. We describe the approach in detail below.

4.1 Training phase

As mentioned earlier, the input to the training phase is a list of Gujarati words. During this phase, the aim is to obtain optimal split position for each word in the corpus. The optimal split position for each word is obtained by systematic traversal of various modules.

In the first module, a check is performed to see if the input word is already in its stem form. This is accomplished by using a list of stems. Besides being used in training the stemmer, this list of stems is also updated with the new stems learnt correctly at the end of training phase. For the first time that the stemmer is trained, this list is empty. If the word exists in the above mentioned list, the optimal split position will be at the end of the word with suffix as NULL.

In the second module, POS-based stemming is performed. As Gujarati does not have a POS tagger, there had to be some method to determine the POS of a word. Since we had the files which shall be used in the development of the Gujarati WordNet and since they also contained POS information, we created a set of files (hereafter referred to as POS-based files), each containing words of a specific POS. We used these files to decide the POS of the word. Also, as mentioned in section 3, we made files (hereafter referred to as suffix files), each containing suffix list for a specific POS. Thus POS-based stemming i.e., stripping of the corresponding suffixes is performed if the word is found in any of the POS-based files.

In the third module, linguistic rules are applied in order to determine the optimal split position. Each such rule is expressed as a pair of precedent and antecedent, both of which are regular expressions. If any part of the word matches any of the precedents, that part is replaced by the corresponding antecedent and the split position is returned as the length of the new word.

If all the previous module checks fail, as a final resort, take-all-splits of the word is performed (see Figure 1) considering all cuts of the word of length L into stem + suffix, i.e., $w_{1,i} + w_{i+1,L}$, where $1 \leq i < L$. The ranking function that can be used to decide the optimal split position can be derived from Eqn 1.

{$stem_1$+$suffix_1$, $stem_2$+$suffix_2$, …, $stem_L$+$suffix_L$}
પાણીમાં={પ + ◌ાણીમાં, પા + ણીમાં, પાણ + ◌ીમાં, પાણી + માં, પાણીમ + ◌ાં, પાણીમા + ◌ં, પાણીમાં + NULL}

Figure 1. All possible word segmentations for the word પાણીમાં *pāṇīmā̃* 'in_water' which has પાણી *pāṇī* 'water' as its stem and માં *mā̃* 'in' as its suffix

The function used for finding the optimal split position must reflect the probability of a particular split since the probability of any split is determined by frequencies of the stem and suffix generated by that split. Hence, probability of a split can be given by Eqn 1 below.

$$P(Split_i) = P(stem = w_{1,i}) * P(suffix = w_{i+1,L}) \quad \text{(Eqn 1)}$$

i: split position (varies from 1 to L)
L: length of the word

Taking *log* on both sides of Eqn 1 and ignoring the constant terms, we get,

$$log(P(Split_i)) = log(freq(stem)) + log(freq(suffix)) \quad \text{(Eqn 2)}$$

The frequency of shorter stems and suffixes is very high when compared to the slightly longer ones. Thus, Eqn 3 is obtained from Eqn 2 by introducing the multipliers i (length of stem) and L-i (length of suffix) in the function in order to compensate for this disparity.

$$f(i) = i * log(freq(stem)) + (L-i) * log(freq(suffix)) \quad \text{(Eqn 3)}$$

Finally, a split position which maximizes the ranking function given by Eqn 3 is chosen as the optimal split position. Once the optimal split of any word is obtained, the frequencies of the stem and the suffix generated by that

[1] http://www.lancs.ac.uk/fass/projects/corpus/emille/

split are updated. The word list is then iterated and the optimal split position is recomputed until the optimal split positions of all the words do not change any more. The training phase was observed to take four iterations typically. At the end of the training phase, a list of stems and suffixes along with their frequencies is obtained. A list of signatures (see Figure 2) is also obtained, where a signature is a data-structure that provides a mapping between the stem and the suffixes with which that stem appears in the corpus. This list of signatures provides a compact representation of the corpus and can be used in case of a need to retrieve the original corpus.

Signature 1:

{ptr(છોકર)} {ptr(ો), ptr(ા)}

Signature 2:

{ptr(ભારત), ptr(બરફ)} {ptr(NULL), ptr(માં)}

Signature 3:

{ptr(ખા)} {ptr(NULL), ptr(વું)}

Figure 2. A sample signature-list for the words - છોકરો *chokro* 'boy', છોકરા *chokrā* 'boys', ભારત *bhārat* 'India', ભારતમાં *bhāratmā̃* 'in_India', બરફ *baraf* 'ice', બરફમાં *barafmā̃* 'in_ice', ખા *khā* 'eat', ખાવું *khāvũ* 'to_eat'

Based on the approach discussed above, an overview of the training algorithm is shown in Figure 3 below.

Step 1. Check if the word is already in its stem form, if yes, return it as it is, else proceed to Step 2.
Step 2. Check if the word is in any POS-based file, if yes, perform POS-based stemming and return, else proceed to Step 3.
Step 3. Check if a match occurs with any of the linguistic rules, if yes, apply the rule and return, else proceed to Step 4.
Step 4. Perform take-all-splits on the word and obtain the optimal split position based on Eqn 3.
Step 5. Perform Step 4 through several iterations until optimal split position of all the words remain unchanged.

Figure 3. Overview of training algorithm

4.2 Stemming of any unknown word

For the stemming of any unknown word, a similar set of steps is followed as in the training phase, with the only change in the take-all-splits module, wherein, for any given word, the function given by Eqn 3 is evaluated for each possible split using the frequencies of the stems and the suffixes learnt during the training phase.

Consider that the words કરવું *karvũ* 'to_do', કરીને *karīne* 'after_doing' and કરીશ *karīsh* 'will_do' existed in the training set, then the frequency of the stem કર *kar* 'do' will be high. Now if the unknown word કરવાથી *karvāthī* 'by_doing' appears in the test set, it will be stemmed as કર + વાથી due to the frequencies learnt during training. In contrast to this, if the training set contained the words પાણીમાં *pāṇīmā̃* 'in_water' and ઘરમાં *gharmā̃* 'in_house', the unknown word ટોપીમાં *ṭopīmā̃* 'in_hat' will be split as ટોપી + માં, due to the high frequency of the suffix માં *mā̃* 'in' learnt during training.

5. Our Approach for Derivational Stemmer

Derivation is a process of combining a word stem with grammatical morphemes usually resulting in a word of different class, not necessarily different POS. Derivational morphology deals with derivation of the words either by affixation (For e.g., જવાબદારી *javābdārī* 'responsibility' derived from જવાબદાર *javābdār* 'responsible') or by performing changes at the morpheme boundary (For e.g., ધાર્મિક *dhārmik* 'religious' derived from ધર્મ *dhārm* 'religion').

The task of derivational stemming is that of reducing the derived word to its derivational stem form. The approach for derivational stemming is inspired from the chapter on morphology by Jurafsky and Martin (2009).

Their approach consisted of the following components. However, only two of them were useful in our case.

1. Lexicon: It is a list of stems and suffixes together with some basic information such as POS. The importance of a lexicon is to determine whether the resultant stem is correct or not. But, as there is no

lexicon for Gujarati, the validation of the stem form cannot be accomplished.

2. Morph-tactics: It is a model that explains morpheme ordering i.e., it explains which class of morphemes can follow which other class of morphemes.
   E.g.: બારીમાંથી *bārīmā̃thī* 'from_window' indicates that થી *thī* can follow માં *mā̃* but the other way round is not possible.
   In order to model morph-tactics, Finite State Automata (FSA) accepting different transitions within words are usually used.
3. Orthographic or spelling rules: These are the rules used to handle changes in the words at the morpheme boundary.
   E.g.: ખવડાવવું *khavḍāvvũ* 'to_make_eat' has its stem as ખા *khā* 'eat', but there is no direct way to reflect this transition. So there is a need of spelling or orthographic rule for such words. Example of such a rule is: વડાવ → ◌ા. The way it is applicable in the system is discussed after the algorithm. We have 73 such hand-crafted rules.

The algorithm steps are shown in Figure 4.

Step 1.	Check if any of the orthographic rules match, if yes, apply the rule and proceed, else proceed to step 2.
Step 2.	Check if any substitution rule is matched, if yes, apply the rule and proceed, else proceed to step 3.
Step 3.	Check if any suffix-stripping rule is matched, if yes, apply the rule and proceed, else proceed to step 4.
Step 4.	Check if the resultant word gets accepted by any FSA, if yes, return the word as the stem, else return the word obtained from the previous module as the stem.

Figure 4. Derivational stemming algorithm

For example, the word ખવડાવવું *khavḍāvvũ* 'to_make_eat' is to be stemmed. In the first step, an orthographic rule matches, which specifies that, if ડાવ appears between વ and વું, વડાવ *vḍāv* should be replaced by ◌ા *ā*, resulting into the intermediate form ખાવું *khāvũ* 'to_eat'. Next, step 2 is not applicable. In step 3, the suffix વું *vũ* is a valid suffix for verbs; hence it is stripped off; resulting into ખા *khā* 'eat', which gets accepted by the FSA for verbs in the final step. Thus, ખા *khā* 'eat' is returned as the derivational stem of ખવડાવવું *khavḍāvvũ* 'to_make_eat'.

6. Experiments and Results

We performed various experiments to evaluate the performance of both the inflectional and derivational stemmer using EMILLE Corpus for Gujarati. We extracted around ten million words from the corpus. We obtained 8,525,649 words after filtering out the wrongly spelt words. In order to create the test set, each time we randomly extracted thousand words from the corpus.

6.1 Performance of the inflectional stemmer

The performance of the inflectional stemmer is evaluated based on three factors. The first factor is the accuracy based on the gold standard data, where the gold standard data contains the ideal stems of all the words in the test set manually tagged by us. Accuracy is defined as the percentage of words stemmed correctly. The second factor is the Index Compression Factor (Fox and Frakes, 2003) that shows the extent to which a collection of words is reduced by stemming. ICF is defined as the ratio of difference in number of unique words and number of unique stems to the number of unique words. Finally, the third factor is mean number of words per signature (MW_c) (Fox and Frakes, 2003) that indicates the strength of the stemmer. MW_c is defined as the ratio of the number of unique words to the number of unique stems.

The experiments were aimed at studying the impact of three heuristics: (i) fixing the minimum permissible stem size, (ii) provide unequal weightage to the stem and suffix and (iii) introduce a threshold as a restriction on the minimum number of stems and suffixes to qualify as a signature, known as the stem filter threshold and the suffix filter threshold respectively.

Various experiments were done to study the impact of different combination of these heuristics. This impact is studied in terms of comparison of various factors as discussed above. The results of such experiments are described in the following subsections.

Varying Minimum Stem Size:

Minimum stem size was varied from 1 to 7 and its impact was observed on performance of the lightweight stemmer. The results of this experiment are shown in Table 1.

Min Stem Size	Accuracy (%)	ICF	MW_c
1	**90.7**	0.53	2.11
2	89.9	0.53	2.11
3	84.8	0.52	2.00
4	74.2	0.49	1.90
5	63.5	0.47	1.92
6	52.1	0.49	1.96
7	44.6	0.55	2.22

Table 1. Effect of minimum stem size on performance of the inflectional stemmer

It can be observed that maximum accuracy of 90.7% is obtained by neglecting the restriction on the minimum stem size and the average index compression is 52% which is considerable as far as IR application is concerned.

The results also show that the performance degrades if a restriction is placed on the minimum stem size. The reason may be that when the minimum stem size is increased lots of genuine, but small stems are neglected, leading to a decline in accuracy.

Providing unequal weightage to stem and suffix along-with minimum stem size:

Initially an equal weightage was provided to stem and suffix in Eqn 3 which is responsible for determining the optimal split position of any word. Then Eqn 4 was obtained from Eqn 3 by introducing a parameter 'α' in order to provide unequal weightage to stem and suffix and its effect was observed on performance of the lightweight stemmer.

We used Eqn 4 and varied α along-with varying the minimum stem size. The results are shown in Table 2.

$$f(i) = \alpha * i * \log(freq(stem)) + (1 - \alpha) * (L-i) * \log(freq(suffix)) \quad \text{(Eqn 4)}$$

Min Stem Size	α	Accuracy (%)	ICF	MW_c
1	0.3	90.0	0.51	2.04
	0.5	**90.7**	0.53	2.11
	0.7	87.0	0.51	2.04
2	0.3	89.2	0.51	2.08
	0.5	89.9	0.53	2.11
	0.7	86.6	0.51	2.04
3	0.3	84.7	0.51	2.05
	0.5	84.8	0.52	2.00
	0.7	82.9	0.50	2.03
4	0.3	74.0	0.49	1.96
	0.5	74.2	0.49	1.90
	0.7	73.2	0.48	1.95
5	0.3	63.2	0.46	1.88
	0.5	63.5	0.47	1.92
	0.7	62.5	0.47	1.90

Table 2. Effect of α along with min. stem size on performance of the inflectional stemmer

It can be observed that the maximum accuracy of 90.7% is obtained by neglecting the restriction on the minimum stem size and providing equal weightage to stem and suffix by keeping α = 0.5. Even for this combination of heuristics, the average index compression of 52% is obtained.

Introducing restriction on the number of stems and suffixes to qualify as a signature:

A restriction was placed on the minimum number of stems and the minimum number of suffixes needed in a signature. These numbers are called stem filter threshold and suffix filter threshold respectively.

We varied all the parameters, viz., minimum stem size, α, stem filter threshold and suffix filter threshold. There were two important observations that will be stated below. The results of this experiment are shown in Table 3 below.

The results show how this combination of heuristics improves the quality of stems and suffixes, as well it brings big boost in the Index Compression Factor.

Min Stem Size	α	Thres-hold	Accu-racy (%)	ICF	MW_c
1	0.3	0	90.0	0.51	2.0
		1	85.8	0.88	9.0
		2	87.1	**0.95**	20.3
1	0.5	0	**90.7**	0.52	2.1
		1	88.3	0.89	9.9
		2	87.7	**0.95**	22.4
1	0.7	0	87.0	0.51	2.0
		1	84.9	0.95	22.2
		2	84.8	**0.95**	22.2
2	0.3	0	89.2	0.51	2.1
		1	85.1	0.88	9.0
		2	86.5	**0.95**	20.3
2	0.5	0	89.9	0.52	2.0
		1	87.6	0.89	9.9
		2	86.7	**0.95**	22.4
2	0.7	0	86.6	0.51	2.0
		1	87.6	0.94	19.2
		2	84.1	**0.95**	22.2

Table 3. Effect of varying all three parameters, viz., min. stem size, α and filter threshold on performance of the inflectional stemmer

It can be observed that the maximum accuracy of 90.7% is obtained by neglecting the restriction on the minimum stem size, providing equal weightage to stem and suffix by keeping $\alpha = 0.5$ and ignoring the restriction on the minimum number of stems and suffixes to form a signature.

Another important observation in this experiment was that by restricting the filter threshold to two, we obtain the highest index compression of 95% with a slight decrease in accuracy. This is an excellent result for applications like corpus compression.

6.2 Performance of the derivational stemmer

The performance of the derivational stemmer was evaluated by direct comparison of the stems generated by the system with the ideal stems present in the gold standard data which gave an accuracy of 70.7%.

7. Conclusions and Future Work

We developed two systems for Gujarati language, one performing inflectional stemming and the other performing derivational stemming.

The inflectional stemmer has an average accuracy of about 90.7% which is considerable as far as IR is concerned. Boost in accuracy due to POS based stemming was 9.6% and due to inclusion of the language characteristics it was further boosted by 12.7%. Heuristic with filter threshold set to 2 gives highest index compression of 95% which is extremely good for applications like compression of data.

The derivational stemmer has an average accuracy of 70.7% which can act as a good baseline and can be useful in tasks such as dictionary search or data compression.

The systems possess potential to be used as pre-processing modules for NLP problems other than IR, such as Word Sense Disambiguation, similarity measure, etc.

The limitations of inflectional stemmer can be easily overcome if modules like Named Entity Recognizer are integrated with the system.

In order to elevate the accuracy of the derivational stemmer, the list of substitution, orthographic or suffix-stripping rules can be improved further if needed.

References

Amaresh K. Pandey and Tanveer J. Siddiqui. 2008. An unsupervised Hindi stemmer with heuristic improvements. *Proceedings of the Second Workshop on Analytics for Noisy Unstructured Text Data*, 303:99-105.

Ananthakrishnan Ramanathan and Durgesh D. Rao. 2003. A Lightweight Stemmer for Hindi. *Workshop on Computational Linguistics for South-Asian Languages*, EACL.

Christopher J. Fox and William B. Frakes. 2003. Strength and Similarity of Affix Removal Stemming Algorithms. *Special Interest Group on Information Retrieval Forum*, 37(1):26-30.

Daniel Jurafsky and James H. Martin. 2009. *Speech and Language Processing: An Introduction to Natural Language Processing, Speech Recognition, and Computational Linguistics.* 2nd edition. Prentice-Hall, Englewood Cliffs, NJ.

Donna Harman. 1991. How effective is suffixing? *Journal of the American Society for Information Science*, 42(1):7-15.

Ilia Smirnov. 2008. Overview of Stemming Algorithms. *Mechanical Translation*.

John A. Goldsmith. 2001. Unsupervised learning of the morphology of a natural language. *Computational Linguistics*, 27(2):153-198.

Julie B. Lovins. 1968. Development of a stemming algorithm. *Mechanical Translation and Computational Linguistics*, 11:22-31.

Martin F. Porter. 1980. An algorithm for suffix stripping. *Program*, 14(3):130-137.

Prasenjit Majumder, Mandar Mitra, Swapan K. Parui, Gobinda Kole, Pabitra Mitra, and Kalyankumar Datta. 2007. YASS: Yet another suffix stripper. *Association for Computing Machinery Transactions on Information Systems*, 25(4):18-38.

Pratikkumar Patel, Kashyap Popat and Pushpak Bhattacharyya. 2010. Hybrid Stemmer for Gujarati. *Proceedings of the 1st Workshop on South and Southeast Asian Natural Languages Processing (WSSANLP), the 23rd International Conference on Computational Linguistics (COLING), Beijing*, 51-55.

William St. Clair Tisdall. 1892. *A simplified grammar of the Gujarati language: together with A short reading book and vocabulary.* D. B. Taraporevala Sons & Company, Bombay

Improving Persian-English Statistical Machine Translation: Experiments in Domain Adaptation

Mahsa Mohaghegh
Massey University
School of Engineering and Advanced Technology
Auckland, New Zealand
M.Mohaghegh@massey.ac.nz

Abdolhossein Sarrafzadeh
Unitec
Department of Computing
Auckland, New Zealand
Hsarrafzadeh@unitec.ac.nz

Tom Moir
AUT University
School of Engineering
Auckland, New Zealand
Tom.moir@aut.ac.nz

Abstract

This paper documents recent work carried out for PeEn-SMT, our Statistical Machine Translation system for translation between the English-Persian language pair. We give details of our previous SMT system, and present our current development of significantly larger corpora. We explain how recent tests using much larger corpora helped to evaluate problems in parallel corpus alignment, corpus content, and how matching the domains of PeEn-SMT's components affect translation output. We then focus on combining corpora and approaches to improve test data, showing details of experimental setup, together with a number of experiment results and comparisons between them. We show how one combination of corpora gave us a metric score outperforming Google Translate for the English-to-Persian translation. Finally, we outline areas of our intended future work, and how we plan to improve the performance of our system to achieve higher metric scores, and ultimately to provide accurate, reliable language translation.

1 Introduction

Machine Translation is one of the earliest areas of research in Natural Language Processing. Research work in this field dates as far back as the 1950's. Several different translation methods have been explored to date, the oldest and perhaps the simplest being rule-based translation, which is in reality transliteration, or translating each word in the source language with its equivalent counterpart in the target language. This method is very limited in the accuracy it can give. A method known as Statistical Machine Translation (SMT) seems to be the preferred approach of many industrial and academic research laboratories, due to its recent success (Lopez, 2008). Different evaluation metrics generally show SMT approaches to yield higher scores.

The SMT system itself is a phrase-based translation approach, and operates using a parallel or bilingual corpus – a huge database of corresponding sentences in two languages.

The system is programmed to employ statistics and probability to learn by example which translation of a word or phrase is most likely to be correct. For more accurate translation results, it is generally necessary to have a large parallel corpus of aligned phrases and sentences from the source and target languages.

Our work is focussed on implementing a SMT for the Persian-English language pair. SMT has only been employed in several experimental translation attempts for this language pair, and is still largely undeveloped. This is due to several difficulties specific to this particular language pair. Firstly, several characteristics of the Persian language cause issues with translation into English, and secondly, effective SMT systems generally rely on large amounts of parallel text to produce decent results, and there are no parallel corpora of appropriate size currently available for this language pair. These factors are prime reasons why there is a distinct shortage of research work aimed at SMT of this particular language pair.

This paper firstly gives a brief background to the Persian language, focusing on its differences to English, and how this affects translation between the two languages. Next, we give details of our PeEn-SMT system, how we developed and manipulated the data, and aligned our parallel corpora using a hybrid sentence aligning method. We give a brief overview of previous tests with the earlier

Proceedings of the 2nd Workshop on South and Southeast Asian Natural Language Processing (WSSANLP), IJCNLP 2011, , pages 9–15,
Chiang Mai, Thailand, November 8, 2011.

version of the system, and then show our latest experiments with a considerably larger corpus. We show how increasing the size of the bilingual corpus (training model), and using different sizes of monolingual data to build a language model affects the output of PeEn-SMT system. We focus on the aim for a general purpose translator, and whether or not the increase in corpora size will give accurate results. Next we show that with the PeEn-SMT system equipped with different language models and corpora sizes in different arrangements, different test results are presented. We explain that the improved result variations are due to two main factors: firstly, using an in-domain corpus even of smaller size than a mixed-domain corpus of larger scale; secondly, spending much focus on stringent alignment of the parallel corpus. We give an overview of the evaluation metrics used for our test results. Finally, we draw conclusions on our results, and detail our plan for future work.

2 Persian Language Characteristics

Persian is an Indo-European language, spoken mostly in Iran, but also parts of Afghanistan, India, Tajikistan, the United Arab Emirates, and also in large communities in the United States. Persian is also known as Farsi, or Parsi. These names are all interchangeable, and all refer to the one language.

The written Persian language uses an extended Arabic alphabet, and is written from right to left. There are numerous different regional dialects of the language in Iran, however nearly all writing is in standard Persian.

There are several grammatical characteristics in written Persian which differ to English. There is no use of articles in Persian, as the context shows where these would be present. There is no capital or lowercase letters, and symbols and abbreviations are rarely used.

The subject in a Persian sentence is not always placed at the beginning of the sentence as a separate word. Instead, it is denoted by the ending of the verb in that sentence. Adverbs are usually found before verbs, but may also appear in other locations in the sentence. In the case of adjectives, these usually proceed after the nouns they modify, unlike English where they are usually found before the nouns.

Persian is a morphologically rich language, with many characteristics not shared by other languages (Megerdoomian & Laboratory, 2000). This can present some complications when it is involved with translation into *any* other language, not only English.

As soon as Persian is involved with statistical machine translation, a number of difficulties are encountered. Firstly, statistical machine translation of the Persian language is only recently being exploited. Probably the largest difficulty encountered in this task is the fact that there is very limited data available in the form of bilingual corpora.

The best language to pair with Persian for machine translation is English, since this language is best supported by resources such as large corpora, language processing tools, and syntactic tree banks, not to mention it is the most widely used language online, and in the electronic world in general.

When compared to English however, Persian has many differing characteristics, some of which pose significantly difficult problems for the task of translation. Firstly, compared to English, the basic sentence structure is generally different in terms of syntax. In English, we usually find sentence structure in its most basic form following the pattern of "subject – verb – object", whereas in Persian it is usually "subject – object – verb". Secondly, spoken Persian differs significantly from its written form, being heavily colloquial, to a much greater degree than English is. Thirdly, many Persian words are spelled in a number of different ways, yet all being correct. This in particular poses trouble for translation, since if one version of the spelling is not found in a bilingual corpus, such a word may be incorrectly translated, or remain as an OOV (out of vocabulary) word. Any SMT system designed for this language pair needs to take these details into consideration, and specifics of the system developed to cater for these differences.

3 PeEn-SMT Compositions

3.1 SMT System Architecture

The goal of a statistical machine translation system is to produce a target sentence $\boldsymbol{e}$ from a source sentence $\boldsymbol{f}$. It is common practice today to use phrases as translation units (Koehn et al., 2003; Och and Ney 2003) in the log-linear frame in order to introduce several models explaining the translation process.

The SMT paradigm relies on the probabilities of source and target words to find the best translation. The statistical translation process is given as:

$$\mathbf{e}^* = \underset{\mathbf{e}}{\operatorname{argmax}} \Pr(\mathbf{e}|\mathbf{f})$$

$$= \underset{\mathbf{e}}{\operatorname{argmax}} \sum_{\mathcal{A}} \Pr(\mathbf{e}, \mathcal{A}|\mathbf{f}) \quad (1)$$

$$\approx \underset{\mathbf{e}}{\operatorname{argmax}} \max_{\mathcal{A}} \Pr(\mathbf{e}, \mathcal{A}|\mathbf{f}) \quad (2)$$

In the above equations, ($\mathcal{A}$) denotes the correspondence between source and target words, and is called an alignment.

The Pr(e, $\mathcal{A}$ |f) probability is modeled by combination of feature functions, according to maximum entropy framework (Berger, Pietra, & Pietra, 1996)

$$\Pr(\mathbf{e}, \mathcal{A}|\mathbf{f}) \propto \exp \sum_i \lambda_i f_i(\mathbf{e}, \mathcal{A}|\mathbf{f}) \quad (3)$$

The translation process involves segmenting the source sentence into source phrases *f*; translating each source phrase into a target phrase *e*, and reordering these target phrases to yield the target sentence **e***. In this case a phrase is defined as a group of words that are to be translated (Koehn, Och, & Marcu, 2003; Och & Ney, 2003) A phrase table provides several scores that quantize the relevance of translating *f* to *e*.

The PeEn-SMT system is based on the Moses SMT toolkit, by (Koehn, et al., 2007). The decoder includes a log-linear model comprising a phrase-based translation model, language model, a lexicalized distortion model, and word and phrase penalties. The weights of the log-linear interpolation were optimized by means of MERT(Och & Ney, 2003). In addition, a 5-gram LM with Kneser-Ney (Kneser & Ney, 2002) smoothing and interpolation was built using the SRILM toolkit (Stolcke, 2002).

Our baseline English-Persian system was constructed as follows: first word alignments in both directions are calculated with the help of a hybrid sentence alignment method. This speeds up the process and improves the efficiency of GIZA++ (Och & Ney, 2000), removing certain errors that can appear with rare words. In addition, all the experiments in the next section were performed using a corpus in lowercase and tokenized conditions. For the final testing, statistics are reported on the tokenized and lower-cased corpora.

3.2 Data Development

For optimum operation, a statistical language model requires a significant amount of data that must be trained to obtain proper probabilities. We had several Persian monolingual corpora available completely adapted to news stories, originating from three different news sources – Hamshahri (AleAhmad, Amiri, Darrudi, Rahgozar, & Oroumchian, 2009), IRNA[1] and BBC Persian[2] – Hamshahri contains around 7.3 million sentences, IRNA has almost 5.6 million, and the BBC corpus contains 7,005 sentences.

It is currently common to use huge bilingual corpora with statistical machine translation. Certain common language pairs have many millions of sentences available. Unfortunately for Persian/English , there is a significant shortage of digitally stored bilingual texts, and finding a corpus of decent size is a critical problem.

One English-Persian parallel text corpus we obtained consisted of almost 100,000 sentence pairs of 1.6 million words, and was mostly from bilingual news websites. There were a number of different domains covered in the corpus, but the majority of the text was in literature, politics, culture and science. Figure.1 shows the corpus divided into separate domains. To the best of our knowledge, the only freely available corpus for the English-Persian language pair is the TEP corpus, which is a collection of movie subtitles consisting of almost 3 million sentences - 7.8 million words. These two corpora were concatenated together to form News Subtitle Persian English Corpus (NSPEC) a single corpus of 3,100,000 sentences for use in one test, and will also be used in the future for further experiments.

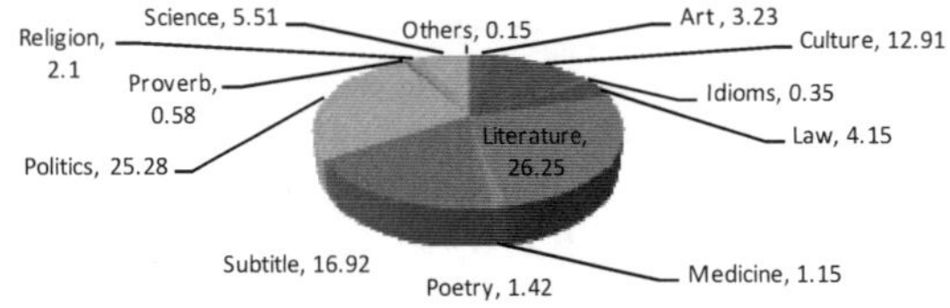

Figure 1. Domain percentages for NSPEC corpus

[1] http://www.irna.ir/ENIndex.htm
[2] http://www.bbc.co.uk/persian/

3.3 Alignment

The issue of word alignment in parallel corpora has been the subject of much attention. It has been shown that sentence-aligned parallel corpora are useful for the application of machine learning to machine translation, however unfortunately it is not usual for parallel corpora to originate in this form. The alignment of the corpus became a task of paramount importance, especially due to the shortage of bilingual text for English-Persian in the first place. There are several methods available to perform this task. Characteristics of an efficient sentence alignment method include speed, accuracy and also no need for prior knowledge of the corpus or the two languages. For the experiments presented in this paper, we used a hybrid sentence alignment method using sentence-length based and word-correspondence based models that covered all these areas, only requiring the corpus to be separated into word and sentence. In each of our experiments we firstly aligned the corpus manually using this hybrid method, and then later using GIZA++ when the data was put through Moses.

4 Experiments and Results

4.1 Overview of Previous Experiments

The original tests performed using PeEn-SMT as shown in some of previous papers produced unsatisfactory results (Mohaghegh, Sarrafzadeh, & Moir, 2010). It was initially thought that this was due to the small corpora and training models used. As detailed in these papers, a number of preliminary tests were carried out, and each time the language model was increased in size to a maximum of 7005 sentences. The training model at its largest consisted of 2343 sentences. The language model in these tests consisted of text collected from BBC news stories, and the training model consisted of a bilingual corpus of mostly UN news. It was thought that the unsatisfactory test results achieved could be remedied by enlarging the language model and corpus, since the amounts of data in each model were far too small to achieve any decent success in SMT.

4.2 Experiments

In order to develop the translation model, an English-Persian parallel corpus was built as explained in the Data Development section. We divided the parallel corpus into different sized groups for each test system. The details of the corpus size for each test are shown in Table 1. Table 2 shows the size of each test's corpus after the text was tokenized, converted to lowercase, and stripped of blank lines and their correspondences in the corpora. This data was obtained after applying the hybrid sentence alignment method.

Language Pair En-Pe	Data Genre	English Sentences	English words	Persian sentences	Persian Words
System1	Newswire	10874	227055	10095	238277
System2	Newswire	20121	353703	20615	364967
System3	Newswire	30593	465977	30993	482959
System 4	Newswire	40701	537336	41112	560276
System 5	Newswire	52922	785725	51313	836709
TEP	Subtitle	612086	3920549	612086	3810734
NSPEC	Newswire -Subtitle	678695	5596447	665678	5371799

Table 1: Bilingual Corpora Used to Train the Translation Model

Language Pair En-Pe	Data Genre	English Sentences	English Words	Persian sentences	Persian Words
System1	Newswire	9351	208961	9351	226759
System2	Newswire	18277	334440	18277	362326
System3	Newswire	27737	437871	27737	472679
System 4	Newswire	37560	506972	37560	548038
System 5	Newswire	46759	708801	46759	776154
TEP	Subtitles	612086	3920549	612086	3810734
NSPEC	Newswire Subtitle	618039	5370426	618039	5137925

Table 2: Bilingual Corpora after Hybrid Alignment Method

We divided the corpus to construct five different systems, beginning from 10,000 sentences in the smallest corpus, and increasing in steps of approximately 10,000 sentences each time up to the 5th test system, with a corpus of almost 53,000 sentences. In addition to the news stories corpus as shown earlier, we only had access to one freely available corpus, and this consisted of movie subtitles in Persian and English. This was shown to be in a completely different domain to our main corpus, so for most cases we preferred to run tests separately when using these corpora. Finally in NSPEC, we concatenated these two corpora, to ascertain the potential output with a combined corpus. We tested the subtitle corpus separately because we wished to see how an out-of-domain corpus affected the result. In all cases, the test set consisted of a news article covering a variety of different domains showing various grammatical aspects of each language. In order to construct a language model, we used the transcriptions and news paper stories corpora. One source we used was the Hamshahri corpus, extracted from the Hamshahri newspaper, one of the most popular daily newspapers in Iran in publication for more than 20 years. Hamshahri corpus is a Persian text collection that consists of 700Mb of news text from 1996 to 2003. This corpus is basically designed for the classification task and contains more than 160,000 news articles on a variety of topics. Another source used was the IRNA corpus, consisting of almost 6 million sentences collected from IRNA (Islamic Republic News Agency). Table 3 summarizes the monolingual corpora used for the construction of the language model. SRILM toolkit (Stolcke, 2002)was used to create up to 5-gram language models using the mentioned resources. We tested the baseline PeEn-SMT system against different sizes of aligned corpora and different sized language models. Tables 4, 5 and 6 show the results obtained using the BBC, Hamshahri, and IRNA language models respectively.

Monolingual	Data Genre	Sentences	Words
BBC	News	7005	623953
Hamshahri (V.1)	News	7288643	65937456
IRNA	News	5852532	66331086

Table 3: Monolingual Corpora Used to Train the Language Model

4.3 Evaluation Metrics

One aspect of Machine Translation that poses a challenge is developing an effective automated metric for evaluating machine translation. This is because each output sentence has a number of acceptable translations. Most popular metrics yield scores primarily based on matching phrases in the translation produced by the system to those in several reference translations. The metric scores mostly differ in how they show reordering and synonyms.

In general, BLEU is the most popular metric used for both comparison of Translation systems and tuning of machine translation models (Papineni, Roukos, Ward, & Zhu, 2002); most systems are trained to optimize BLEU scoring. Many alternative metrics are also available however. In this paper we explore how optimizing a selection of different evaluation metrics effect the resulting model. The metrics we chose to work with were BLEU, IBM-BLEU, METEOR, NIST, and TER. While BLEU is a relatively simple metric, it has a number of shortcomings.

There have been several recent developments in evaluation metrics, such as TER (Translation Error Rate). TER operates by measuring the amount of editing that a human would have to undertake to produce a translation so that it forms an exact match with a reference translation (Snover, Dorr, Schwartz, Micciulla, & Makhoul, 2006).METEOR (Denkowski & Lavie, 2010; Lavie & Denkowski, 2009) is a metric for evaluating translations with explicit ordering, and performs a more in-depth analysis of the translations under evaluation. The scores they yield tend to achieve a better correlation with human judgments than those given by BLEU (Snover, et al., 2006).

Another metric used was IBM-BLEU (Papineni, et al., 2002) , which performs case-insensitive matching of n-grams up to n=4.

BLEU and NIST (Zhang, Vogel, & Waibel, 2004) both produce models that are more robust than that of other metrics, and because of this, we still consider them the optimum choice for training.

4.4 Evaluation of the Results

Our first experiment was carried out with 10,000 sentences (System1) in the English-to-Persian translation direction. For comparison we tested the SMT model on different language models. As shown in Tables 4, 5, and 6, the best result was achieved when we trained the machine on the IRNA language model. We gradually increased the size of the corpora to the next test set (System 2), which was almost 21,000 sentences, and we repeated the test for different language models. Again the result showed that using IRNA resulted in the best translation, followed by BBC, then Hamshahri. We observed almost identical trends with each test set; up to the set with the largest corpus (53,000 sentences, System 5). It was originally thought that the dramatic increase in the size of both models would yield a much higher metric score, since it gave the translation program more data to work with. However, these new tests proved that this was not necessarily always true, and corpus size alone was not synonymous with improved translation. For instance, in the case where the Hamshahri corpus was used for the language model, the output result was even worse than the original tests with a far smaller corpus like BBC. The IRNA corpus, larger than the original BBC corpus (7005 sentences) but still smaller than Hamshahri, yielded the best result of the two.

To establish a reason for the apparently illogical test results, the characteristics of each corpus were examined, together with their combinations in each test. After analysis, it was seen that there were a number of likely factors contributing to the poor results.

	Language Model =BBC news					
	Evaluation					
System	BLEU_4	MULTI_BLEU	IBM-BLEU	NIST	METEOR	TER
System 1	0.1417	10.96	0.0083	2.4803	0.3104	0.7500
System 2	0.1700	12.63	0.0172	2.5258	0.3347	0.6287
System 3	0.2385	24.66	0.0242	3.4394	0.3654	0.6312
System 4	0.2645	25.45	0.0274	3.6466	0.4466	0.6515
System 5	0.2865	26.88	0.0467	3.8441	0.4479	0.8181
TEP	0.1312	10.56	0.0095	2.6552	0.2372	0.8333
NSPEC	0.2152	19.94	0.0453	3.2643	0.3929	0.6824

Table 4: Automatic Evaluation Metrics of PeEn-SMT

	Language Model =Hamshahri					
	Evaluation					
System	BLEU_4	MULTI_BLEU	IBM-BLEU	NIST	METEOR	TER
System 1	0.1081	7.60	0.0246	2.1453	0.2526	0.8106
System 2	0.1229	8.77	0.0300	2.4721	0.3078	0.7196
System 3	0.1325	10.73	0.0149	1.2080	0.2215	0.7236
System 4	0.1945	10.87	0.0303	2.4804	0.2970	0.7500
System 5	0.2127	11.25	0.0288	3.6452	0.3040	0.8863
TEP	0.0127	1.05	0.0219	1.2547	0.1377	0.9015
NSPEC	0.0856	7.15	0.0499	1.9871	0.2313	0.7825

Table 5: Automatic Evaluation Metrics of PeEn-SMT System

	Language Model =IRNA					
	Evaluation					
System	BLEU_4	MULTI_BLEU	IBM-BLEU	NIST	METEOR	TER
System 1	0.2472	19.98	0.0256	3.5099	0.4106	0.6969
System 2	0.3287	29.47	0.0636	4.0985	0.4858	0.5833
System 3	0.3215	29.37	0.0565	4.1409	0.4838	0.5606
System 4	0.3401	30.99	0.0565	4.2090	0.4833	0.5833
System 5	*0.3496*	*29.25*	*0.0635*	*4.4925*	*0.5151*	*0.5236*
TEP	0.0535	3.98	0.0301	1.8830	0.2021	0.8787
NSPEC	0.1838	12.87	0.0366	3.0264	0.3380	0.7234

Table 6: Automatic Evaluation Metrics of PeEn-SMT System

One such factor involved the *nature* of the data comprising each corpus, and how this affected the match between the language model and the training model. For instance, in the case where we achieved an even lower score than the original tests, it was noted that the training model consisted of a bilingual corpus based mainly on *movie subtitles*, yet the Hamshahri corpus was a collection of *news stories*. For the most part, movies consist of spoken, natural language in everyday situations, filled with idioms, colloquial expressions and terms, and often incorrect grammar and sentence structure. These characteristics were heavily present in the training model. News stories on the other hand not only ideally consist of well-structured sentences, with correct grammar and little presence of colloquialism, but the very nature of this kind of literature is unique, and rarely found in natural language.

Another example showing this involved the subtitle corpus (TEP) that we had access to. This corpus was significantly larger in size (612,000 sentences) when compared to the other corpora that we had available to us. However, when we performed the same experiment against different language models, the result was quite unsatisfactory. We believe that this was due to our test sets being in a different domain than that of the movie subtitles.

These results led us to conclude that using larger language and training models alone was not a reliable determining factor in satisfactory output.

For the sake of comparison, Google Translator was tested on the same test data and results are included in Tables 7. We compared our system to Google's SMT for this language pair, and compared to the evaluation metric score released by Google. Our PeEn-SMT system outperforms the Google translator in the English-to-Persian translation direction.

Google (English – Persian)						
System	BLEU_4	MULTI_BLEU	IBM-BLEU	NIST	METEOR	TER
Google	0.2611	21.46	0.0411	3.7803	0.5008	0.7272

Table 7: Automatic Evaluation Metric of Google Translator Output

5 Conclusion and Future Work

In this paper we presented the development of our English/Persian system PeEn-SMT. This system is actually a standard phrase-based SMT system based on the Moses decoder. The originality of our system lies mostly in the extraction of selected monolingual data for the language model. We used manual alignment of the parallel corpus, which was a hybrid sentence alignment method using both sentence length-based and word correspondence-based models, the results of which prove this method to be invaluable in obtaining a more accurate result from the system. We showed that increasing the size of the corpus alone cannot necessarily lead to better results. Instead, more attention must be given to the domain of the corpus. There is no doubt that the parallel corpora used in our experiments are small when compared to other corpora used in training SMT systems for other languages, such as German and Chinese, etc, or with Google, which has access to extensive resources. However we believe that the results from our system compare quite favorably, despite these shortcomings which we intend to address in our future work.

In the future we plan to develop a technique to find the most appropriate corpus and language model for PeEn-SMT system by detecting the domain of the input. We intend to perform tests using the matched-domain input, corpus and language models in an attempt to achieve even better translation results.

References

AleAhmad, A., Amiri, H., Darrudi, E., Rahgozar, M., & Oroumchian, F. (2009). Hamshahri: A standard Persian text collection. *Knowledge-Based Systems, 22*(5), 382-387.

Berger, A., Pietra, V., & Pietra, S. (1996). A maximum entropy approach to natural language processing. *Computational Linguistics, 22*(1), 39-71.

Denkowski, M., & Lavie, A. (2010). Meteor-next and the meteor paraphrase tables: Improved evaluation support for five target languages.

Kneser, R., & Ney, H. (2002). *Improved backing-off for m-gram language modeling.*

Koehn, P., Hoang, H., Birch, A., Callison-Burch, C., Federico, M., Bertoldi, N., et al. (2007). *Moses: Open source toolkit for statistical machine translation.*

Koehn, P., Och, F., & Marcu, D. (2003). *Statistical phrase-based translation.*

Lavie, A., & Denkowski, M. (2009). The METEOR metric for automatic evaluation of machine translation. *Machine translation, 23*(2), 105-115.

Lopez, A. (2008). Statistical machine translation.

Megerdoomian, K., & Laboratory, N. M. S. U. C. R. (2000). *Persian Computational Morphology: A unification-based approach*: Computing Research Laboratory, New Mexico State University.

Mohaghegh, M., Sarrafzadeh, A., & Moir, T. (2010, 2010). *Improved Language Modeling for English-Persian Statistical Machine Translation.* Paper presented at the Proceedings of SSST-4, Fourth Workshop on Syntax and Structure in Statistical Translation,Coling, Beijing.

Och, F., & Ney, H. (2000). *Improved statistical alignment models.*

Och, F., & Ney, H. (2003). A systematic comparison of various statistical alignment models. *Computational Linguistics, 29*(1), 19-51.

Papineni, K., Roukos, S., Ward, T., & Zhu, W. (2002). *BLEU: a method for automatic evaluation of machine translation.*

Snover, M., Dorr, B., Schwartz, R., Micciulla, L., & Makhoul, J. (2006). *A study of translation edit rate with targeted human annotation.*

Stolcke, A. (2002). *SRILM-an extensible language modeling toolkit.*

Zhang, Y., Vogel, S., & Waibel, A. (2004). *Interpreting BLEU/NIST scores: How much improvement do we need to have a better system.*

Thai Word Segmentation Verification Tool

Supon Klaithin Kanyanut Kriengket Sitthaa Phaholphinyo Krit Kosawat
Human Language Technology Laboratory, National Electronics and Computer Technology Center, National Science and Technology Development Agency
112 Thailand Science Park, Klong Luang, Pathumthani 12120, Thailand
{supon.kla, kanyanut.kri, sitthaa.pha, krit.kos}@nectec.or.th

Abstract

Since Thai has no explicit word boundary, word segmentation is the first thing to do before developing any Thai NLP applications. In order to create large Thai word-segmented corpora to train a word segmentation model, an efficient verification tool is needed to help linguists work more conveniently to check the accuracy and consistency of the corpora. This paper proposes Thai Word Segmentation Verification Tool Version 2.0, which has significantly been improved from the version 1.0 in many aspects. By using hash table in its data structures, the new version works more rapidly and stably. In addition, the new user interfaces have been ameliorated to be more user-friendly too. The description on the new data structures is explained, while the modification of the new user interfaces is described. An experimental evaluation, in comparing with the previous version, shows the improvement in every aspect.

1 Introduction

Thai is an isolating language; each word form consists typically of a single morpheme. There are no clearly defined boundaries of words and sentences; for example, "คนขับรถ" /kh-o-n^-0/ kh-a-p^-1/r-o-t^-3/ can refer to two references: "a driver" or "a man drives a car", which may be considered as a compound word or a sentence, depending on its context. Therefore, creating an NLP application that involves Thai language processing is more complicated than many other languages, such as English, Malay, Vietnamese, etc., in which word boundaries are clearly defined.

Moreover, Thai word segmentation research has been separately conducted in many academic institutes for more than 20 years without common standard. Their word boundary definitions, segmentation methods and training/test data, etc. are usually incompatible and nonexchangeable. That is why a benchmark on their works is rather difficult. As a result, the research in Thai NLP has progressed more slowly than what it should be.

Furthermore, the trend in language processing research has now changed from rule-based approaches to statistical-based ones, which need very large scale annotated corpora to train the system by means of a machine learning technique. Unfortunately, none of such huge resources has been built for Thai (Kosawat *et al.*, 2009).

1.1 BEST Project on Thai word segmentation

BEST project was set up in 2009 to smooth out these problems. BEST or "Benchmark for Enhancing the Standard of Thai language processing" aims to establish useful common standards for Thai language processing in various topics, to organize several contests in order to find the best algorithms by means of benchmarking them under the same criteria and test data, as well as to share knowledge and data among researchers. This strategy is expected to help accelerate the growth of the NLP researches in Thailand (Kosawat *et al.*, 2009; Boriboon *et al.*, 2009).

The BEST project was started with Thai word segmentation (BEST Academy, 2009), in which Thai word-segmented corpora of 8.7 million words had been developed as a training set in 12 balanced genres. The BEST corpora were originally segmented by SWATH (Smart Word Analysis for THai) (Meknavin *et al.*, 1997), applica-

Proceedings of the 2nd Workshop on South and Southeast Asian Natural Language Processing (WSSANLP), IJCNLP 2011, , pages 16–22, Chiang Mai, Thailand, November 8, 2011.

tion of which word segmentation criteria differed from our BEST segmentation guidelines (BEST Academy, 2008). Therefore, it was the laborious works of our linguists to correct any wrongly segmented words, as well as any spelling errors, by hand.

1.2 Previous work

In order to facilitate our linguists to edit the BEST Corpora more conveniently, Word Segmentation Verification Tool Version 1.0 had been created. The program was written in Java language and had many useful features as follow:

- It could open simultaneously many text files, so we could work with several texts in the same time.
- It could accept text encoding both in UTF-8 and TIS-620 (Thai ASCII).
- Word list with word frequency was provided, as well as word concordance.
- Search and replace functions were available.
- Content editor was provided.

However, the version 1.0 had some disadvantages, such as:

- It needed a powerful PC with a large size memory.
- Opening many files still caused a very long delay and sometimes a system halt.
- Its interface was not user-friendly.
- Quite a few bugs were reported.

That is why we decided to develop a new version of Word Segmentation Verification Tool. This new program has been changed in many fields, which will be described in the next section.

2 Word Segmentation Verification Tool Version 2.0

To verify the accuracy and consistency of the BEST corpora, we need an efficient program that works fast and is easy to use. So, we have developed "Word Segmentation Verification Tool Version 2.0" to reduce the time to work with a lot of files.

2.1 System architecture overview

The new tool is composed of three main components: File manipulation, Word list manipulation and Content manipulation, as shown in Figure 1.

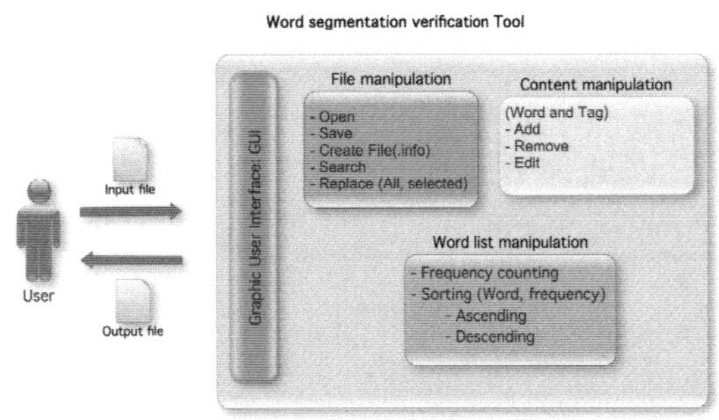

Figure 1. System architecture

- File manipulation: the module that handles text files. It can handle one or multiple files. The program begins by reading files and storing them in the data structure. It also includes related works, such as creating files, finding and replacing words in files.
- Word list manipulation: a word frequency analysis on text files. This module counts the frequency of words and displays the list of words sorted by alphabet or frequency in ascending or descending order.
- Content manipulation: responsible for content and tag modification in text files. This module contains several functions such as add, remove and edit tag. The result of these modifications will immediately effect the content of the file. But the original file is saved as a backup before.

2.2 Work flow

Word Segmentation Verification Tool V2.0 accepts an input text file in TIS-620 or UTF-8 encoding. This program can read multiple files. Because the program is a tool to validate Thai word segmentation, the input files must be word-separated by pipe symbol "|", as shown in Figure 2.

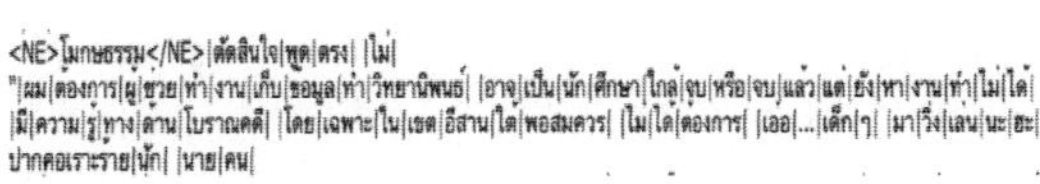

Figure 2. Word boundaries with pipe symbol

After successfully reading input files, the tool will count all words, calculate word frequencies and store the full path of the file names and line numbers of words in a data structure. The information, containing word position, line number and file name, will be displayed on the main interface, along with word concordance, when a word is selected from the word list. When user selects a line from the concordance, another window will appear and allow user to edit its content. A backup file (.info) is created before saving the new content in the original file. The operation's work flow is shown in Figure 3.

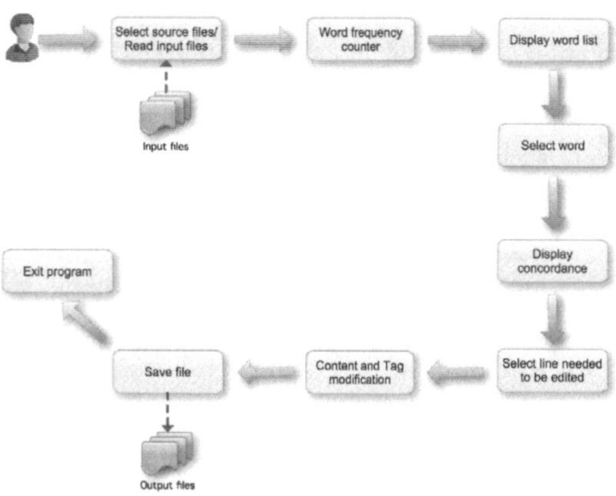

Figure 3. Work flow

Other significant functions in the main interface are search and replace functions. These functions find the word positions in every opened file. All search results are displayed to user to select a replacement. There are two types of replacement: replace only selected line, or replace all (every word in all opened files).

2.3 Data structure

A hash table is a data structure that uses a hash function to identify the values in array elements (buckets). The advantage of hash table is the ability to fast access the data in the large scale of corpus (Wikipedia, 2011). So, we have decided to use the hash table in our new application.

The data structure of "Word Segmentation Verification Tool V2.0" is stored in the hash table format. The file path is stored as a key in the hash table to identify its value. The content of the file is stored in a vector, which is the value of the hash table. The vector stores the content by sorting it from the first line to the last line. For example, Figure 4 shows that "C:/input/file1" is stored as a key and Vector1, which contains all lines of file1, is stored as a value in Hashtable1.

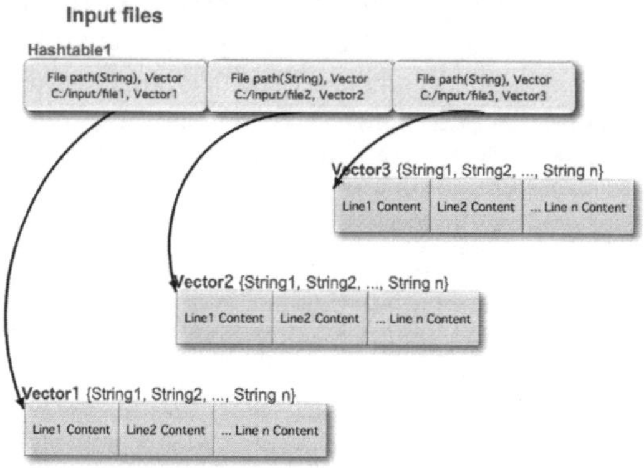

Figure 4. Data structure of input files

In addition, the frequency of each word is collected in another hash table as shown in Figure 5. Hashtable2 stores the word as a key and the address of its child hash table as a value. The data structure of the child hash table is similar to the data structure of Figure 4 but different in vector elements, since the actual vector elements contain line number and frequency of word in that line.

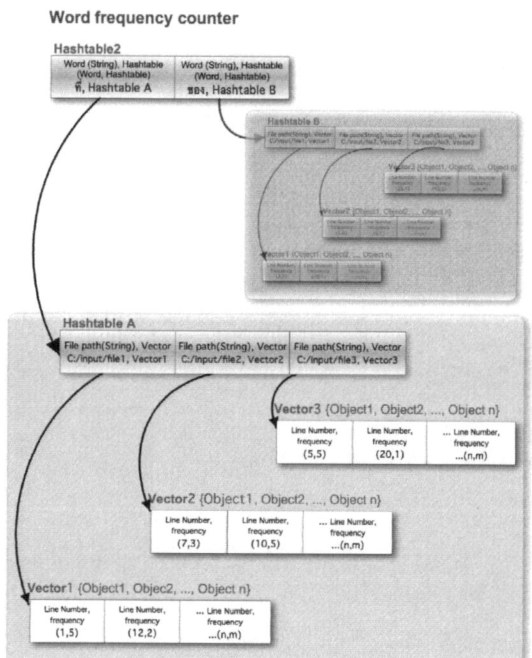

Figure 5. Data structure of word frequency counter

2.4 Program interfaces

Main interface

We have developed a new main interface to be easy to use. This interface consists of four main components as follows:

- Word list - this section is quite useful to quickly explore words, frequency of words, and word segmentation's correctness. It counts the frequency of words from all opened files. The result displayed in this section can be sorted by alphabet or by frequency in ascending or descending order.

- Concordance display - this section is very important and helpful for linguists to immediately judge which words are correctly segmented by glancing over their contexts, so it is not necessary to open every file to examine each line thoroughly. When a word is selected from the word list or user enters a keyword in the search function, the program will display the result in this section. This section shows the word positions in all opened files by highlighting the target word apart from its contexts. The line numbers and file names of that word are also shown. By double-clicking at the content of each line, another window will appear to edit data, as will be described in the next section.

- Search and Replace - this operation is the most frequently used function in our tool. It is an important component of the main interface. This function allows user to easily search and replace words. The result of each search is displayed in the concordance table. There are two options for replacement; the first is replacing only in the selected line(s), and the second option is replacing in all opened files. For adding a tag into the data, there are three options: merge, split and none.

- Finally, Tag history - it displays tag list that has been modified in the data. It shows which words were edited by merging, splitting, or tagging any special symbols. This history can help users remind any former word segmentation modifications in order not to commit the same errors again.

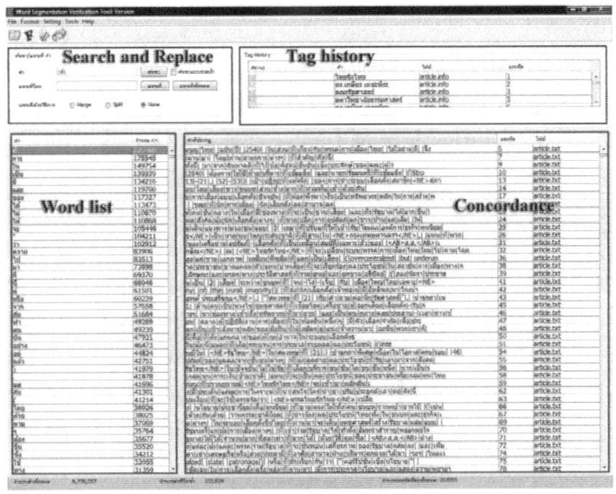

Figure 6. Main interface

Particular interface

The particular interface is the second part of the software interfaces for editing misspelled and wrongly segmented words or texts thoroughly, and also marking words or texts with some tags to notify some particular structures or word ambiguities. An example of the particular interface's dialog box is shown below.

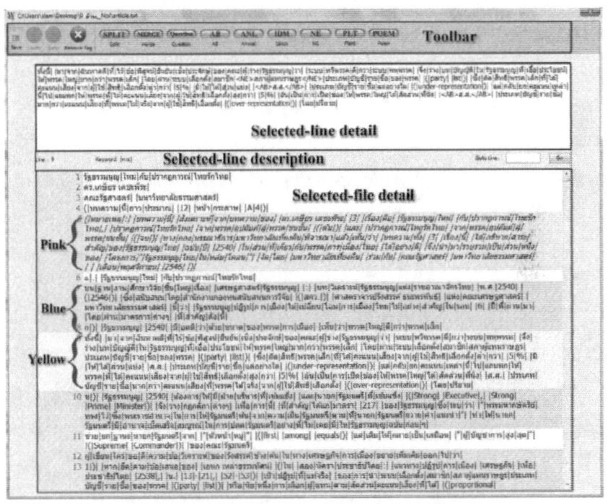

Figure 7. Particular interface

According to the above figure, the window has four parts: Toolbar, Selected-line detail, Selected-line description, and Selected-file detail. The first part is the toolbar consisting of several editing and tagging menus: Save, Undo, Redo, Remove tag, and nine symbols of tagging, which will be explained in the part of tag editor. The second part is the selected-line detail showing all words and tags which appear in the selected line. In this part, all words can be manually edited and tagged with symbols. The third part is the selected-line description showing the line number and the keyword of the selected line. Moreover, in this part, users can change the selected line by filling any line number in the box on the right side. Finally, the last part is the selected-file detail showing all words and tags which appear in the file of the selected line. Each line in the file is highlighted differently to show the line status. Any lines without editing are not highlighted. The selected line is highlighted in yellow. Any lines having the keyword are highlighted in blue. Lastly, any edited lines are highlighted in pink with italic characters. The particular interface is very useful for editing texts more correctly.

Tag editor

Tag editor is the last part of the software interfaces to notify any special structures of words or texts. Due to the fact that BEST corpora are composed of several text genres with various word structures inside, the tag editor is used to mark any words or texts having particular structures or ambiguities. Since the corpora, which were originally segmented by machine, have some mistakes, the tag editor is used to edit the corpora correctly, as well. There are nine symbols to use for the mentioned purposes.

Firstly, the symbol <QUESTION>...</QUESTION> is used to mark any ambiguous words or texts which have various meanings or are still in discussion. When linguists analyze them with their contexts to clarify the appropriate meanings, then the symbols will be removed, and the words will be segmented, split, or tagged with other symbols as the experts have already considered.

Secondly, the symbols <MERGE>... </MERGE> and <SPLIT>...</SPLIT> are used to mark any words edited by being merged or split in order not to segment them wrongly again. The first one is used to tag the words that are correctly edited by being merged together because, originally, at least two words were automatically segmented despite having to be combined[1]. The next one is used to tag the words that are correctly edited by being split because, formerly, at least two words were automatically combined together despite having to be divided.

Lastly, six symbols are used to mark any words or texts having particular structures, which are quite different from general word formation, in order to manage them extraordinarily. These symbols are <AB>...</AB> for abbreviations, <ANL>...</ANL> for animal names and breeds, <IDM>...</IDM> for idioms, aphorisms, proverbs and sayings, <NE>...</NE> for named entities, <PLT>...</PLT> for plant names and breeds, and <POEM>...</POEM> for poems, verses and poetry. Some examples are shown in the table below.

Words	Word tagging
400 ก.ม. (400 km.)	400 <AB>ก.ม.</AB>
ปลากัด (fighting fish)	<ANL>ปลากัด</ANL>
ถ่านไฟเก่า (old lover)	<IDM>ถ่านไฟเก่า</IDM>
กรุงเทพมหานคร (Bangkok)	<NE>กรุงเทพมหานคร</NE>
พริกชี้ฟ้า (goat pepper)	<PLT>พริกชี้ฟ้า</PLT>
อ้ายเข้อ้ายโขง อยู่ในโพรงไม้สัก	<POEM>อ้ายเข้อ้ายโขง อยู่ในโพรงไม้สัก</POEM>

Table 1. Examples of word tagging

3 Experimental evaluation

According to the development of Word Segmentation Verification Tool, the performance of the latest version is evaluated by doing an experiment on both previous and latest versions of the tools. They are tested on a desktop computer[2] with 113-MB corpora, containing 880 files or 8,778,357 words in total. The corpora are composed of general words, abbreviations, animal names and breeds, idioms, named entities, plant names and breeds, poems, numbers and punctuation marks. It is found that the latest version is mainly improved in two aspects: time and user friendly.

The first aspect is time usage. The latest version of the software spends less time opening the software, files and keywords. In general, both versions spend almost equal time opening the software for the first time. However, for the latest version, every time opening the software is faster because it will open only the software, and then, users have to open files; on the contrary, for the previous version, if it is not the first time opening the software, it will take much time to open the software together with any files which were opened before closing the software.

[1] Any words being merged or split depend on the linguistic rules in the BEST guidelines.

[2] The test computer is a Personal Computer (PC) with Intel Core 2 Duo 3.0 GHz. processor and 2 GB RAM, and using Microsoft Windows XP operating system.

Round	Previous version (min:sec:ms[3])	Latest version (min:sec:ms)
1	01:15:01	00:56:04
2	01:15:06	00:57:04
3	01:14:04	00:56:04
4	01:15:08	00:57:00
5	01:14:08	00:57:00

Table 2. Time usage of opening files after firstly opening the software

According to the above table, the latest version works faster. To open the test corpus files (880 files containing 8,778,357 words), it took almost 1 minute; on the contrary, the previous version spent about 1 minute 15 seconds doing it. Furthermore, the latest version is also much quicker than the previous one to show the lines containing the selected keywords with contexts, as shown in the table below. The latest version could immediately display the lines of the required keyword while the previous one had to spend several seconds doing it. Also, more often the keywords were chosen to display, more slowly the previous version worked. In conclusion, the software's latest version works much quicker than the old one.

Round	Previous version (sec:ms)	Latest version (sec:ms)
1	15:02	immediately
2	16:09	immediately
3	15:03	immediately
4	17:09	immediately
5	18:00	immediately

Table 3. Time usage of showing lines containing the selected keywords with contexts

The second aspect is user friendly. The latest version of the software is easier and more convenient. Firstly, it can work faster because it is not necessary to spend much time opening the files which is used to open before closing the program like the previous version, as told in the first aspect. Secondly, the function of asking to segment any long lines, which is a function of the previous version (as shown in Figure 8 below), is not necessary for this latest version anymore because the new version can completely manage any long lines without problem.

[3] min = minute; sec = second; ms = millisecond

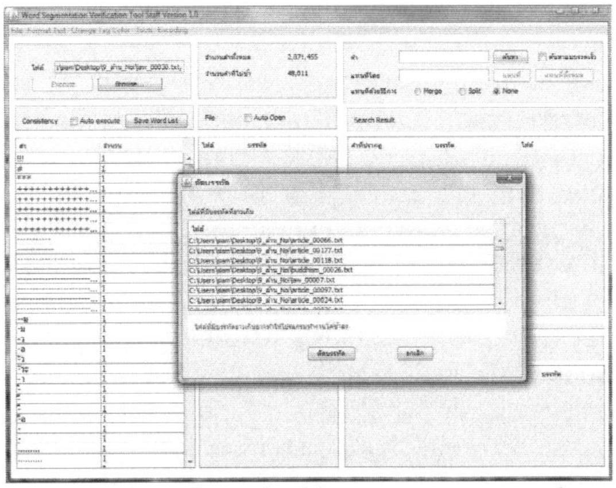

Figure 8. Function of asking to segment any long lines in the previous version

Thirdly, the main interface of the latest version looks easier to use because it contains only essential and necessary components: word list, concordance display, search and replace, and tag history (as explained in the main interface part). In contrast, the main interface of the previous one contained a useless component (shown in the bold square). It presented file names and lines of selected words, both of which also occurred in the concordance component. Moreover, the useless component caused fewer space to display the word contexts in the concordance component. Therefore, it was inconvenient for linguists to quickly know which words were segmented correctly. The useless component of the main interface of the previous version is shown in Figure 9 below.

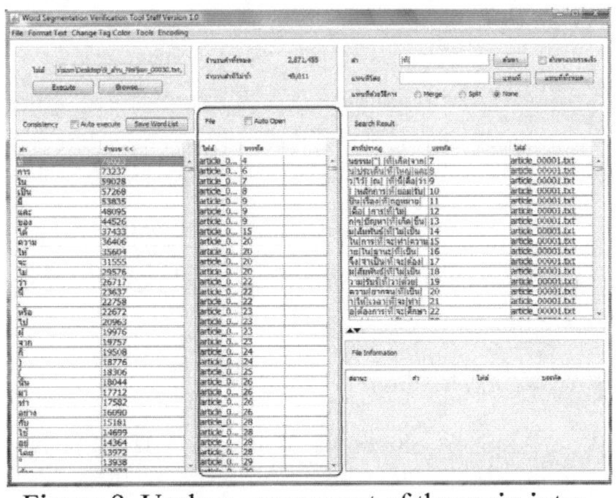

Figure 9. Useless component of the main interface of the previous software version

Fourthly, it is easier to approach the data by one click; in contrast, double click is used for reaching the data in the previous software version.

Lastly, user knows the status of the software. During the software's execution, every button, such as editing, searching and saving buttons is inactive, and a pop-up message and status-bar message show the software's working status. It is quite safe and useful for users not to edit or search other words during this time because they know that the software has not finished working yet and is not ready to do other functions. On the other hand, when it finishes working, every button is active and ready to use again, and the pop-up message displays the number of edited words. It is very helpful for users because they will know when to be able to edit words, and not to correct the corpus during the software's execution. If not, the corpus will have full of errors, and it will waste plenty of time to revise the corpus again and again. Therefore, the software's latest version has much improvement and is quite appropriate to the linguists' usage.

4 Conclusion and future works

We showed that our new tool, with its new data structures in the form of hash table, worked more rapidly than the previous version, both for opening files and for responding to users. Moreover, finding and replacing function were very quick and stable too, for it never caused a system halt again. The new interface was more user-friendly. We can say that the overall improvement of the new program can help our linguists work more happily. In consequence, the BEST Corpora can be enlarged in a shorter period while their data follow better to the word segmentation standard guidelines too.

In the near future, we plan to integrate Thai spelling checker in our tool to detect automatically any misspelled words. Moreover, making use of word statistics to decide how to segment words, especially words still in discussion (marked with <QUESTION> tag), may be another interesting function to help our linguists pass their stressful days.

References

BEST Academy. 2008. "Guidelines for BEST 2009 : Thai Word Segmentation Software Contest (Release4) (in Thai)." [online]. Available at: http://thailang.nectec.or.th/2009/

BEST Academy. 2009. "BEST 2009 : Thai Word Segmentation Software Contest." [online]. Available at: http://thailang.nectec.or.th/2009/

Monthika Boriboon, Kanyanut Kriengket, Patcharika Chootrakool, Sitthaa Phaholphinyo, Sumonmas Purodakananda, Tipraporn Thanakulwarapas, and Krit Kosawat. 2009. "BEST Corpus Development and Analysis." In *Proceedings of the 2nd International Conference on Asian Language Processing, IALP 2009*. the IEEE Computer Society, Singapore:323-327.

Krit Kosawat, Monthika Boriboon, Patcharika Chootrakool, Ananlada Chotimongkol, Supon Klaithin, Sarawoot Kongyoung, Kanyanut Kriengket, Sitthaa Phaholphinyo, Sumonmas Purodakananda, Tipraporn Thanakulwarapas, and Chai Wutiwiwatchai. 2009. "BEST 2009 : Thai Word Segmentation Software Contest." In *Proceedings of the 8th International Symposium on Natural Language Processing, SNLP 2009*. Dhurakij Pundit University, Thailand:83-88.

Surapant Meknavin, Paisarn Charoenpornsawat, and Boonserm Kijsirikul, 1997. "Feature-based Thai Word Segmentation." In *Proceedings of the Natural Language Processing Pacific Rim Symposium 1997(NLPRS'97)*, Phuket, Thailand.

Wikipedia. 2011. "Hash table." [online]. Available at: http://en.wikipedia.org/wiki/Hash_table

The Semi-Automatic Construction of Part-Of-Speech Taggers for Specific Languages by Statistical Methods

Tomohiro YAMASAKI **Hiromi WAKAKI** **Masaru SUZUKI**
Toshiba Corp., Corporate Research & Development Center, Knowledge Media Laboratory
1. Komukai Toshiba-cho, Saiwai-ku, Kawasaki, JAPAN
{tomohiro2.yamasaki, hiromi.wakaki, masaru1.suzuki}@toshiba.co.jp

Abstract

Economic activities now keep being globalized more and more. Thus we are driven to deal with not only the documents written in English but also those written in other languages. In order to enable us to develop processors of any language quickly, we have been making a framework based on statistical processing and machine learning. At present, we confirmed that part-of-speech (POS) taggers of some target languages can be built by using this framework and the information of source languages. In this paper, we describe the method of acquiring POS lexicons and that of generating supervisors of POS sequences, which are used to learn grammatical models of target languages. We also explain the experimental results of building POS taggers of Portuguese and Indonesian by using some source languages.

1 Introduction

The natural language processing, for example, part-of-speech (POS) tagging, syntactic parsing, and named entity extraction, is the fundamental technology for information extraction from text documents. This means that the preparation of processors of a specific language enables us to develop various applications for that language such as keyword extraction, document classification, and machine translation. However, most parts of the processors we have already built are dependent on the characteristics of each language since we have developed lexicons and grammars manually according to those of target languages such as Japanese and English. This means that we have to spend much time and effort when we try to prepare processors of a new language in the similar way before.

On the other hand, economic activities keep being globalized and thus we should provide people all over the world with appropriate services and products. In particular, the following needs are increasing:

- to estimate customers' concerns and intentions in order to provide the best service,
- to grasp customers' reputations and complaints in order to avoid troubles,
- and to analyze the documents written in local languages in order to achieve two above-mentioned statements.

We have mainly worked on processing of English until now, since many people tend to consider to be international as to use English much. After now, however, we must work on not only English but also other languages all over the world in order to be *truly* international.

Therefore, we have been working on the establishment of the framework that enables us to develop processors of any language quickly. Concretely speaking, we aim to build lexicons and grammatical models semi-automatically by using statistical processing. We also aim to achieve processors for POS tagging and more advanced language processing by using only the combination of surface and statistical information of documents given. However, we make it a condition that the documents written in target languages have many translations with source languages because it is difficult to build processors without any clue at all.

Roughly speaking, the technical points of our research are divided into the development of lexicons and that of grammatical models. In

Proceedings of the 2nd Workshop on South and Southeast Asian Natural Language Processing (WSSANLP), IJCNLP 2011, , pages 23–29,
Chiang Mai, Thailand, November 8, 2011.

this paper, we choose POS taggers as an example of processors and describe the method of the following processes:

- to acquire POS lexicons that are composed of [word, POS] pairs,
- to generate supervisors of POS sequences,
- and to learn grammatical models by using the above-mentioned lexicons and supervisors.

As a result of these processes, we can obtain the POS tagger of the target language semi-automatically. Finally, we do the experiment of building POS taggers by using some source languages and evaluate the accuracy of those taggers.

1.1 Related Work

Recently, it has been found that various problems of tasks in the natural language processing can often be solved easily by machine learning if we can prepare a large amount of tagged corpora. However, it is a large problem to prepare tagged corpora that can be used as supervisors of each task.

On the other hand, it is easy to obtain raw corpora from the Internet and so on. Therefore, there are some studies about the methods for building processors by using not tagged corpora but only raw ones. (Goldsmith, 2001) acquires the inflections of each word on the basis of Minimum Description Length (MDL) model. However, in order to use the method of (Goldsmith, 2001), we first have to generate probabilistic grammars manually, because this method is to distinguish the ones acceptable and the ones not acceptable. This means that we have to know the characteristics of the target language well to some degree, and that it is difficult to build processors of the language we hardly know by this method.

In addition, semi-supervised learning is receiving much attention as the method for solving the problem of preparing a large amount of tagged corpora in these days. This is a method aiming to obtain the same effect as the case where we prepare a large amount of tagged corpora by giving only a small amount of tagged data to a large amount of raw corpora. (Niu et al., 2003) learns the extraction rules from the seed words given first, generates the corpora of named entities by those rules, and finally builds a named entity extractor. As to semi-supervised learning, however, it is known that if tagged data include errors even a little, errors increase rapidly in the phase of automatic generation of supervisors and thus it is difficult to achieve enough accuracy. It is also difficult to give data with accurate tags when we hardly know the target language. Therefore, we have to do trial and error so as not to cause the error propagation.

1.2 Policy

When we use translations with some specific languages, the degree of difficulty of obtaining them has a big influence on us. Generally speaking, major news websites often deliver not only articles written in local languages but also those written in English. In other words, there is a large probability that the documents written in local languages have the English translations, which we can use as parallel corpora. However, we note that even if we can obtain the translations with languages X and Y, the sentences within the translations do not always have one-to-one relations. Generally speaking, it is difficult to associate the sentences of language X with the sentences of language Y with high accuracy when we hardly know the relations of words of both languages. Much less, it is almost impossible when we hardly know the target languages.

Therefore, we decided to use the translations of the Bible as our experimental corpora. The Bible is one of the most familiar documents that are read all over the world and the translations with many languages are open to the public on the Internet ((The Unbound Bible,)). In addition, the number of chapters and sections are the same in any language though each translation of the Bible is partitioned into many chapters and sections. This means that the sentences have almost one-to-one relations because each section has few sentences.

On the other hand, as we described above, we aim to achieve processors for advanced language processing by using only the combination of surface and statistical information of documents given. As the first approach, we decided not to target the languages as follows:

- the languages whose character system has not been digitalized yet,

- the languages whose words are not written with a space between them,
- and the languages whose orthographies do not distinguish common nouns and proper nouns.

Not only the languages that have very few users but also some of those that are used in India are known that their character systems have not been digitalized yet. We cannot disregard those Indian languages because they have many users, but we cannot perform the computer statistics if there is no digitalized corpora. Next, Thai, Cambodian, and Laotian languages are known that their words are not written with a space between them. These languages, similar to Japanese, have a large problem that it is very difficult for computers to divide a sentence into words. Then, Arabic, Hebrew, and Hindi languages have no case sensitivity. These languages, similar to German whose nouns always start with capital letters, have difficulties to extract the relations of words of other languages because it is not easy to determine proper nouns.

For these reasons, we mainly target the languages that use Latin characters. Particularly in this paper, we consider Portuguese and Indonesian as major targets. However, our method can be applied also to other languages like French and Italian.

2 Extracting the relations of words

Our method for acquiring POS lexicons is composed of two processes. One is a process of extracting useful words by using statistics of only one language. The other is a process of extracting the relations of words of two languages by using statistics of both languages. In this section, we describe both processes.

2.1 Extracting useful words on the basis of statistical information of a single language

Here, we describe the process of extracting the words whose surfaces are similar to one another (say sim-set), proper nouns, and word collocations on the basis of statistical information of a single language. The purpose of extracting sim-sets is to presume the inflections/derivations of each word at the next process.

As we described in Section 1.2, we consider Portuguese and Indonesian as major targets. This means that the words that always start with capital letters must be proper nouns, though we have to take into account the words that appear at the beginning of sentences. Therefore, we partition all sentences with spaces and symbols into words and extract each word w that satisfies the following conditions from them:

- $c_{small}(w)$, which is the count that w has only small letters, is equal to 0.
- $c_{capital}(w)$, which is the count that w starts with capital letters, is greater than or equal to 5.

The probability that a word that is not a proper noun satisfies the condition $c_{small}(w) = 0$ and $c_{capital}(w) \geq 5$, is less than $(1/2)^5 = 1/32$ even if we assume that the probability that it appears at the beginning of sentences is 1/2. It follows that we can decide whether a word is a proper noun with significance level of 5%.

Next, C-value (Frantzi and Ananiadou, 1996) is known well as a method for extracting word collocations from the text documents. This method calculates the connectivity between the words, defined as $C - value(\mathbf{w}) = (l-1)(n - t/c)$, where $\mathbf{w}$ is a word collocation $w_1 \ldots w_l$, t and c are the total count and the distinct count of word collocations that include $\mathbf{w}$ and that are longer than $\mathbf{w}$.

When the connectivity between some words is strong, these words often appear composing a group and C-value tends to be large because t tend to be small in comparison with n. However, when the word collocations is short, C-value tends to be unreasonably large because c tends to be very large in comparison with n. Therefore, we use not only C-value but also C'-value (Yamasaki, 2008) in order to extract word collocations. In other words, we extract the word collocations whose C-value and C'-value are larger than a threshold given.

Here, Portuguese is classified into the inflectional language grammatically as well as other European languages. The inflectional languages have the property that the elements of grammatical functions are embedded in each word and thus each word changes its form according to the case, the gender, and the number. This means that we must have the means

Table 1: Example of french words extracted from the French Bible

Proper nouns	Word collocations	Sim-sets
Jubal	en paix	{répara,réparer,réparé,réparât,
Assyrie	le livre	réparent,réparèrent},
Jébusien	car vous	{sanctifie,sanctifie-la,sanctifier,sanctifié,
Guérar	nos pères	sanctifieras,sanctifiée,anctifiez-vous,
Nimrod	l'autel	sanctifierai,sanctifierez,sanctification,
Calakh	de guerre	sanctifiés,ssanctifièrent,sanctifiez-le,
Gaza	sa femme	sanctifiez,sanctifiaient,sanctifient,
Dikla	d'Égypte	sanctifiait,sanctifieront,sanctifiât}

by which we can determine inflection forms of each word. Indonesian is classified into the agglutinative language as well as Japanese. The agglutinative languages have the property that most words are formed with the joint of the elements of grammatical functions. This means that we must have the means by which we can determine the stem of derivation words.

In most languages, it is known that the beginning or the end of each word change its form, though the middle does in Arabic and Hebrew. Therefore, we formally define a sim-set as the words whose common affix is longer than a threshold given. Now, we partition all sentences with spaces and symbols into words and perform the following process for each pair of words (w_1, w_2):

- let L, l be max, min of $(|w_1|, |w_2|)$, respectively.
- define $w_1 \sim w_2$ if and only if $l \geq L/2$ and the length of common prefix $pre(w_1, w_2) \geq L/2$ or the length of common suffix $suf(w_1, w_2) \geq L/2$.
- partition all words into equivalence class based on $\sim^*$, which is defined as the reflexive transitive closure of $\sim$.

We note that the definition of $\sim^*$ does not depend on the definition of $\sim$. This means that if we define $\sim$ by using common subsequence instead of common affix, we may apply the same method to the languages where the middle of each word changes.

2.2 Extracting the relations of words on the basis of statistical information of two languages

Here, we describe the process of extracting the relations of words of two languages on the basis of statistical information of both languages.

We expect that when a word w^x of language X corresponds to a word w^y of language Y, the positions of w^x in corpora are related to those of w^y. Here, we note that it is not easy to decide whether the positions have any relations because the sentences within the translations do not always have one-to-one relations. However, it is easy to do it when we use the translations of the Bible because the sentences are almost parallel. Assume that an X–Y parallel corpus has n corresponding sentences and that the numbers of sentences where w^x and w^y appear are shown in Table 2. For example, both appear in a sentences, only w^x (w^y) in b (c), and neither in d.

For such a table, it is known that χ^2-value, defined as $\chi^2 = n(ad - bc)^2/efgh$, follows a χ^2 distribution. On the basis of this value, we can decide whether the words correspond to each other. In addition, we can also decide the relations of 2-grams and those of word collocations in the same way, because this test uses only the number of sentences and does not depend on the characteristics of languages and the length of each sentence. On the other hand, because this test does not use the information where the word appears in a sentence, we sometimes obtain two or more words that correspond to a word given. This does not matter so much if we can finally acquire POS lexicons composed of [word, POS] pairs. However, in order to extract one-to-one relations in any case, we make it a condition that we select the most similar one in the similarity of surfaces. This is because a proper noun is probably pronounced similarly in any language. In that sense, it is more general to calculate the similarity after we convert the surface into the pronunciation.

Now, we have described the method of extracting words and their relations by using not language dependent information but sta-

Table 2: The number of sentences where w^x and w^y appear

	w^y appears	w^y does not appear	sum
w^x appears	a	b	$e = a + b$
w^x does not appear	c	d	$f = c + d$
sum	$g = a + c$	$h = b + d$	$n = a + b + c + d$

tistical information. From here, on the assumption that we know language X well (= we have a POS tagger of language X), we describe the method of extracting the inflections/derivations of words of language Y we hardly know.

As we described in the previous section, a sim-set includes candidates of inflection/derivation forms of a word. Because we have a POS tagger of language X, we can decide whether some different words are in truth the same by restoring each word to its standard form. In other words, we can extract inflection/derivation forms of language Y that correspond to a standard form of language X by finding the subset that is contained in a sim-set of language Y and is the most relevant to the standard form of language X. Therefore, we perform the following processes:

- choose a standard form of language X $\overline{w^x}$ and a sim-set of language Y $sim^y = \{w_1^y, w_2^y, \ldots\}$.
- calculate χ^2-value for each subset $\overline{sim^y}$, which is contained in sim^y.
- find the subset whose χ^2-value is maximum.

3 Acquiring POS lexicons and generating supervisors of POS sequences

In the previous section, we explained the method of extracting the relations of words of languages X and Y on the basis of statistical information obtained from X–Y parallel corpora. In order to acquire POS lexicons of language Y finally, it is necessary to estimate the POS of each word w^y of language Y. Because we can know the POS of each word w^x of language X on the assumption that we have a POS tagger of language X, we consider the POS of w^x corresponding to w^y as that of w^y.

Here, we note that we may not be able to decide the unique POS of w^x. For example, it is known that many English words are used as a NOUN and a VERB. In other words, most of English words have two or more POSes. While the English word "name" can be used as a NOUN and a VERB, the Portuguese word "nome" is used as a NOUN only. Therefore, from the viewpoint of the relevance ratio, it is thought to be better that we estimate POSes on the basis of the context. However, in order to make our method simple, we consider all possible POSes of w^x as those of w^y.

Table 3: List of part-of-speeches

A	ADJECTIVE	P	PRONOUN
C	CONJUNCTION	R	ADVERB
D	DETERMINER	S	PREPOSITION
I	INTERJECTION	V	VERB
M	NUMERAL	0	DIGIT
N	NOUN	_	SYMBOL

It is known well that most of European languages belong to Indo-European languages and there are few differences in the fundamental grammars between them. Conversely speaking, this means that the difference of languages does not affect so much the POS sequences of the corresponding sentences. Though Indonesian does not belong to Indo-European languages, we generate the supervisors of POS sequences of language Y on the basis of POS sequences of language X by solving the Minimum Cost Matching Problem that has the following conditions:

- the POSes of D, P, S, 0 and _ can match the same POSes only, which is because these POSes are thought to be the same POSes for other languages,
- the skip cost is c_{skip},
- the match cost is 0 if $cand(w^y) = \emptyset$ or $pos(w^x) \in cand(w^y)$, otherwise c_{diff},

where $pos(w^x)$ is the POS of a word w^x of language X and $cand(w^y)$ is the POS candidates of a word w^y of language Y.

For example, Figure 3 shows that the French word "commencement" matches the English word " beginning" and thus is estimated to

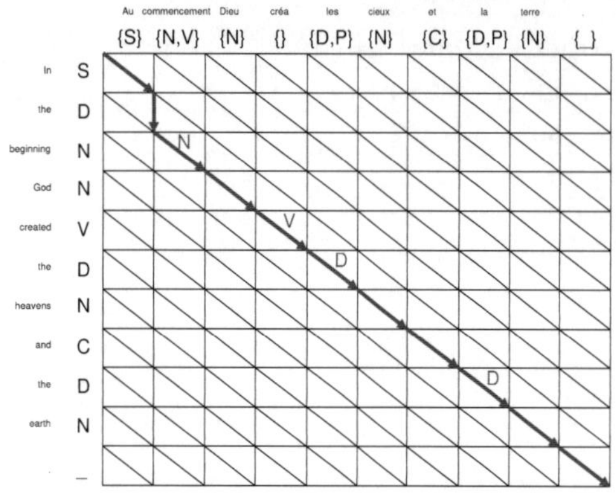

Figure 1: A solution of Minimum Cost Matching Problem solved by Dynamic Programing

be a NOUN. It also shows that "créa" matches "created" and thus is estimated to be a VERB. In order to make our method simple, we do not use the relations of words this time. However, we may make the condition that the match cost reflects the relations of words.

4 Experimental results

We have already built the POS taggers of English, Spanish and Esperanto manually. In this section, we explain the experimental results of building POS taggers of some target languages semi-automatically on the assumption that English, Spanish and Esperanto are used as the source languages. While there are some versions of the Bible by different translators in some languages, we used the following versions shown in Table 4 on this experiment.

First, we show the covering ratios in Figure 2. The total and distinct covering ratios are defined as the ratios of total and distinct words with one or more estimated POSes by using our method, respectively. Though there are a few differences, as you can see, the covering ratios in Figure 2 are almost the same degree even if the source language is English, Spanish or Esperanto.

This means that our method is stable and is independent of the characteristics of source languages. In addition, we confirmed that we acquired the POSes to almost all words by using statistical processing because the total covering ratio exceeds 0.8. However, the distinct covering ratio of Indonesian is about 0.25 and is lower than expected. There is still room for improvement.

Next, we generated the supervisors of POS sequences based on the above-mentioned POS lexicons and performed the machine learning of grammatical models by using CRF (Laffert, 2001). After that, we obtained the POS taggers of the target languages semi-automatically. We show the accuracy ratio in Figure 3. The accuracy ratio is defined as the ratio of correct POSes that the taggers tagged onto words of sentences given. As you can see, POS information is not attached to the Bible. In order to evaluate the accuracy ratio, we extracted about 60 sentences (about 900 words) from the Bible and made the POS answers manually. Figure 3 shows that the Portuguese tagger achieved high accuracy of about 0.9 even though they are built semi-automatically. Figure 3 also shows that the accuracy of the Indonesian tagger is about 0.6. This is probably because the differences between Indonesian and source languages are large.

On the other hand, we analyzed failure cases and confirmed that one of the causes of incorrect POSes that the taggers tagged is to reflect grammatical features of source languages. For one example, the word "there" in English is ADVERB but is often expletive. For this rea-

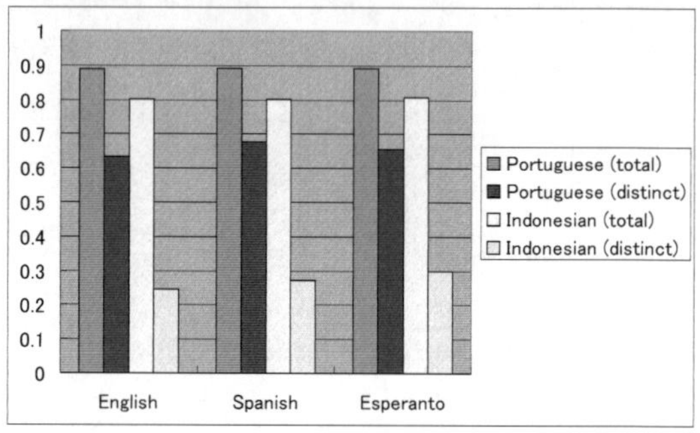

Figure 2: Total and distinct covering ratios

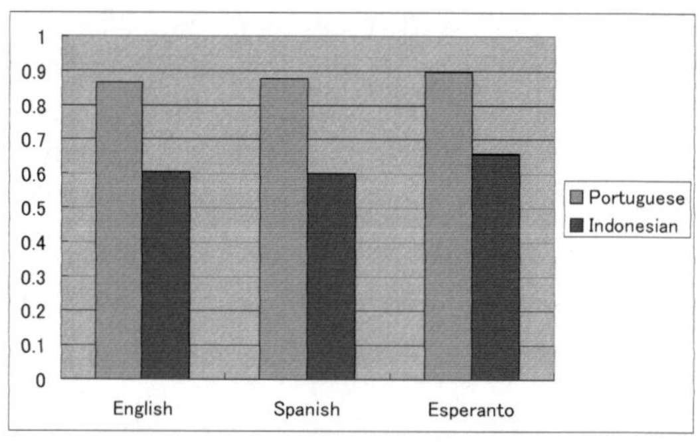

Figure 3: The accuracy ratios of POS taggers

Table 4: List of languages and versions of the Bible

Language	Version	Sections	Total words	Distinct words
English	American Standard	31103	918287	13256
Spanish	Reina-Valera	31103	824760	28874
Esperanto	British and Foreign Bible Society	31103	796700	30760
Portuguese	João Ferreira de Almeida	31103	828352	29306
Indonesian	Bahasa Indonesia Sehari-hari	31103	765810	47947

son, our taggers sometimes predicted by mistake some words as ADVERB, though those words should be NOUN in Portuguese and Indonesian. For another example, ADJECTIVE comes ahead of NOUN in English although ADJECTIVE comes behind NOUN in Portuguese and Indonesian. For this reason, at the sequences of words with the possibility of being ADJECTIVE and NOUN, our taggers sometimes predicted the previous word as ADJECTIVE as if the English tagger does.

Well, as you can easily see, many words that do not appear in the Bible appear in modern documents. This brings us a worry that the accuracy ratio might drop in proportion to the drop of the covering ratios, because as to the words that do not appear in the POS lexicons, our taggers must predict POSes from only peripheral words. Therefore, it will be important to develop the method of extracting modern words and estimating their POSes from large corpora such as Wikipedia documents, for example, by using grammatical knowledge of target languages given by hand at the minimum.

5 Conclusion

In this paper, we described our method that is composed of two following processes. One is the process of acquiring POS lexicons that are composed of [word, POS] pairs by using parallel corpora of source languages and target languages. The other is the process of generating supervisors that are used for machine learning of grammatical models. And we confirmed that Portuguese and Indonesian POS taggers are built semi-automatically by using the Bible as parallel corpora and by using English, Spanish and Esperanto as the source languages. In addition, we confirmed that the Portuguese tagger achieved high accuracy of about 0.9 while the accuracy of the Indonesian tagger is about 0.6.

Although we did not target the languages that use Cyrillic characters and Greek characters in this paper, we have a mind to expand the coverage of our method to such languages as Russian, Ukrainian and Greek in the future. On the other hand, a method (Mochihashi et al., 2009) has attracted a great deal of attention from many researchers in these years. This method partitions each sentence into words by using only statistical information of the documents given. We will work on word segmentation and will expand the coverage of our method to the languages which are not written with a space between words.

References

Biora University. 2005. *The Unbound Bible.* `http://unbound.biola.edu/`.

C. Niu, W. Li, J. Ding, R.K. Srihari. 2003. *A bootstrapping approach to named entity classification using successive learners.* Proc. of 41st Annual Meeting of ACL, pp.335–342, July 2003.

J. Goldsmith. 2001. *Unsupervised learning of the morphology of a natural language.* Journal of Computational Linguistics (2001), vol.27, no.2, pp.153–198.

K.T. Frantzi and S. Ananiadou. 1996. *Extracting nested collocations.* COLING-96, pp.41–46.

T. Yamasaki. 2008. *Topic extraction from Electronic Program Guides by using decomposition of the co-occurrence graph into strongly connected components.* Journal of Computational Linguistics (2001), vol.27, no.2, pp.153–198.

J. Laffert. 2001. *Conditional random fields: Probabilistic models for segmenting and labeling sequence data.* Proc. of Machine Learning (2001), pp.282–289.

D. Mochihashi, T. Yamada, N. Ueda. 2009. Bayesian unsupervised word segmentation with nested Pitman-Yor language modeling. ACL '09 Proceedings of the Joint Conference of the 47th Annual Meeting of the ACL and the 4th International Joint Conference on Natural Language Processing of the AFNLP, vol.1, pp.100-108.

Towards a Malay Derivational Lexicon: Learning Affixes Using Expectation Maximization

Suriani Sulaiman, Michael Gasser, Sandra Kübler
Indiana University
{ss23,gasser,skuebler}@indiana.edu

Abstract

We propose an unsupervised training method to guide the learning of Malay derivational morphology from a set of morphological segmentations produced by a naïve morphological analyzer. Using a morphology-based language model, we first estimate the probability of a given segmentation. We train the model with EM to find the segmentation that maximizes the probability of each morpheme. We extract the set of affix patterns produced by our algorithm and evaluate them against two references: a list of affix patterns extracted from our hand-segmented derivational wordlist and a derivational history produced by a stemmer.

1 Introduction

For languages with complex morphology, morphological analysis is a crucial step. In most languages, morphological analyzers built with comprehensive morpho-phonological rules are used to predict properties of words such as part-of-speech (POS) or morpho-syntactic features on the basis of affixes. Designing a morphological analyzer capable of producing a complete analysis requires extensive human effort and there is therefore considerable interest in machine learning of morphology.

In languages where words are not separated by spaces, such as Chinese and Japanese, statistical language modeling and unsupervised learning are the preferred methods of learning segmentation of sentences into words (Ge et al., 1999; Peng and Schuurmans, 2001; Kit et al., 2003). For morphological segmentation, unsupervised methods include the use of minimum description length (Goldsmith, 2001; Creutz and Lagus, 2005), the learning of suffixation operations and derivational rules from an inflectional lexicon (Gaussier, 1999), the application of minimum edit distance and mutual information (Baroni et al., 2002), and the mutation of virtual morphs (Kohonen et al., 2008). Most of these studies focus on well-resourced languages with mostly inflectional morphology such as English, German, and French that usually take no more than one prefix or suffix; the techniques have not been proven to work on an under-resourced language like Malay. The only effort to learn Malay morphology through a corpus based approach that we are aware of is the work of Knowles and Mohd Don (2006) who discovered Malay word classes using a stemmer. Unfortunately, their work lacks a technical discussion of the learning approach, and the origin of the stemmer remains unclear.

In this paper, we adopt a modified version of the unsupervised technique from Chinese word segmentation (Ge et al., 1999; Peng and Schuurmans, 2001; Kit et al., 2003) to learn the derivational morphology of Malay, a language with hardly any inflectional morphology, by manipulating the output of a naïve morphological analyzer. Given a Malay word, the analyzer guesses all its possible morphological segmentations, producing a list of potential hypotheses. We then use the EM algorithm to find the segmentation that maximizes the probability of each morpheme. Finally, we extract the set of all possible affix patterns from the best segmentations and evaluate them against our gold standard. Our task is not to evaluate the performance of the analyzer per se but to collect as many reliable affix patterns as possible with the help of language modeling and EM in an effort to build a Malay derivational morphological lexicon.

The remainder of the paper is organized as follows: Sec. 2 describes the basics of Malay derivational morphology. Sec. 3 presents an overview of the unsupervised learning of morphological segmentation. Sec. 4 discusses results and evaluation and Sec. 5 concludes.

Proceedings of the 2nd Workshop on South and Southeast Asian Natural Language Processing (WSSANLP), IJCNLP 2011, , pages 30–34, Chiang Mai, Thailand, November 8, 2011.

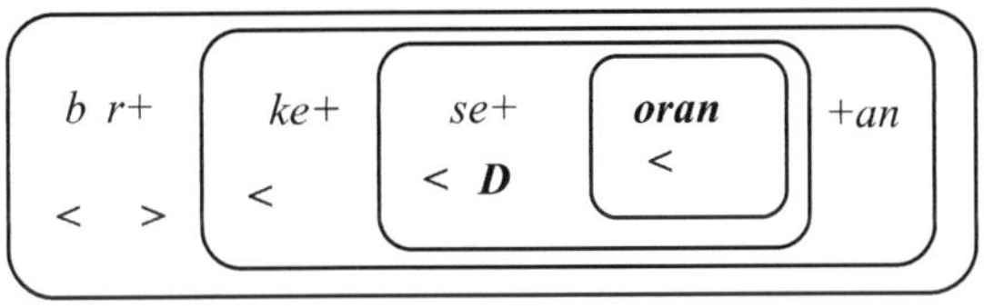

Figure 1: Nested structure of Malay morphology

English:	Malay:
use-**ful-ness**	**per-se**-*faham*-**an**
help*-ness-ful**	**se-per**-*juang*-**an**

Figure 2: English versus Malay morphotactics

2 Malay Derivational Morphology

Malay is an Austronesian language with rich concatenative word structure and productive derivational morphology. A Malay word can be divided into discrete morphemes with clearly defined boundaries, including roots, prefixes, suffixes, infixes, and circumfixes (Knowles and Mohd Don, 2006). In Malay morphology, affixes can be nested, as shown in Figure 1.

The loose restriction on word formation and the productive nature of certain affixes in Malay results in a large number of possible affix patterns, and the nested structures impose complex constraints on how affixes are combined. Unlike in English, some affixes in Malay can be combined in different orders, depending on the roots, to produce derived words with distinct parts-of-speech (Figure 2).

Malay derivational morphology also makes use of reduplication, which is the only non-concatenative feature in Malay for which morpheme boundaries are difficult to handle (Beesley and Karttunen, 2003). In this experiment, we exclude reduplication for the sake of simplicity.

3 Unsupervised Learning of Derivational Morphology

We first extract unique word types from our training corpora and feed them into the Malay morphological analyzer. We then build an n-gram model from the output of the analyzer. For each derived word type, the analyzer provides a list of possible morphological segmentations. However, these are unreliable because of the limitations of the analyzer (see next section). In order to get a better estimate of the probability of each morpheme, we train the n-gram model with EM on a new list of pre-segmented derived word types produced by the same analyzer using larger corpora from a different domain. Finally, the best segmentations are chosen, and unique affix patterns are extracted as initial steps in developing a derivational lexicon.

Malay word:	*diketahui* (Eng.: "*know*")
Hypothesis :	{*di-ketahu-i, di-ketahui, di-ke-tahu-i, diketahui, di-ke-tahui, diketahu-i*}

Figure 3: Sample analysis from Malay analyzer

3.1 MorfoMelayu

We use a finite-state Malay morphological analyzer, MorfoMelayu,[1] provided with an undifferentiated list of about 5000 Malay roots, a list of prefixes, and a list of suffixes. The analyzer is naïve in the sense that it knows no constraints on the order or co-occurrence of affixes. Given an input Malay word, it produces all possible segmentations of the word based on its limited knowledge of the language (Figure 3).

Although this list should include the correct segmentation, it will normally also include an average of five incorrect ones for every word analyzed. It is the task of our machine learning algorithm to learn the precise morphotactics of Malay derivational morphology.

3.2 Morphology-based Language Model

n-gram models are widely used in statistical language modeling to estimate the probability of a character or word sequence. They can be utilized to find the most probable segmentation of a word or sentence. In morphology-based language modeling, morphemes are treated as the modeling unit (Tachbelie, 2010) instead of characters or words. Since Malay morphology is mostly concatenative, it is reasonable to use morphemes as n-gram units. Given a Malay word $w = m_1 m_2 \ldots m_k$, where k represents the number of morphemes, its most likely segmentation into a morpheme sequence can be determined according to maximum likelihood estimation (MLE) as:

$$s(w) = argmax \prod_{i}^{k} p_{ML}(m \mid m_{i-n+1}^{i-1}) \qquad (1)$$

where m_{i-n+1}^{i-1} is the context of morpheme m_i and n the order of the n-gram model. We choose

[1] MorfoMelayu can be downloaded from `https://www.cs.indiana.edu/~gasser/Research/software.html`.

a bigram model for this experiment because it is less likely for a sequence of morphemes than for a single morpheme to coincide with a root. As an example, the Malay prefix sequence *meN-teR* is very likely to be part of a derived word, e.g., *meN-teR-**tawa*** (laugh), while the prefix *teR* alone can easily be part of the root, e.g., *terbang* (fly) or *terjun* (jump). Given a list of pre-segmented Malay derived words from the output of the Malay morphological analyzer, which we refer to as *L-model-news*, we collect the frequency counts of bigram morphemes from each word and estimate their probability:

$$p_{ML}(m_i \mid m_{i-1}) = \frac{f(m_{i-1}, m_i)}{f(m_{i-1})} \quad (2)$$

For smoothing, we apply Jelinek-Mercer linear interpolation, which has been shown to perform well on smaller training sets (Chen and Goodman, 1998) on our n-gram model. We reserve a section of the training corpus for heldout data, *L-heldout-news*, containing 1,303 pre-segmented words containing 2,347 unique bigrams. The bigrams are partitioned into 4 different buckets according to their frequencies and independently trained with the parameter value λ, tuned between 0.1 and 0.9. We linearly interpolate the bigram and unigram model:

$$p_{itp}(m_i \mid m_{i-1}) = \lambda p_{ML}(m_i \mid m_{i-1}) + (1-\lambda) p_{ML}(m_i) \quad (3)$$

where λ is set to 0.1 for low frequency bigrams (0-2 counts), 0.5 for high frequency bigrams (>10 counts) and 0.9 for bigrams of intermediate frequency (3-10 counts). Given that the output of the Malay morphological analyzer is only partially reliable to begin with, we train the bigram model with EM on a different pre-segmented wordlist *L-train-lit* produced by the same analyzer. This step ensures a more reliable $p_{ML}(m_i)$ by minimizing the bias towards the performance of the language model, forcing EM to learn to generalize from the model.

3.3 EM Training

EM is favored mainly due to its guaranteed convergence to a good probability model that locally maximizes the likelihood or posterior probability of the training data (Dempster et al., 1977). In this experiment, given a set of hypotheses for all possible segmentations of a particular word w, $s(w) = \{w'_1, w'_2, \ldots, w'_j\}$, we use EM to find the most probable segmentation that maximizes $s(w)$. Instead of initializing with uniform distribution across the training data, we use the initial probability estimation from the bigram model to boost the slow convergence of EM and perform 10 iterations to produce a more reliable $f(m)$ for estimating $p(m)$ using (4):

$$f^{t+1} = \sum_{w \in L-tr} \sum_{w' \in S(w)} \frac{p^t(w')}{\alpha} f^t(m \in w') \quad (4)$$

where m now represents a sequence of two morphemes, t the current iteration and $f^t(m \in w')$ the number of times a morpheme sequence m occurs in segmentation w'. Since maximum likelihood training is known to penalize longer sequences, we add the normalization factor α in (4), which is the sum of the probabilities of all possible segmentations for a particular word w. We assume a uniform distribution for each unique morpheme in the training list *L-train-lit* and assign$f^0(m)$ a frequency of 1. We adjust (2) as (5) for simplicity, where $f(m)$ is the sum of frequency of all bigrams in *L-model-news*. We derive $p^0(m)$ and its subsequent values from (5).

$$p(m_i) = \frac{f(m_i)}{\sum_{w \in L-model} f(m)} \quad (5)$$

We update the count of each morpheme through (4) for an optimum value of $p(m_i)$. The updated value of $p(m_i)$ is then used to re-calculate $s(w)$ through (1) at the end of each iteration. Note that this differs slightly from the normal implementation of EM in which $s(w)$ is re-estimated at each step. We find that this method speeds up the convergence process and improves the overall performance of EM for our tasks.

3.4 Derivational Lexicon of Affix Patterns

Based on the best segmentations produced by our EM algorithm, we extract all unique affix patterns by combining over possible roots. We then construct a lexicon consisting of unique affix patterns (e.g., *meN-X-kan, ber-ke-X-an*, where *X* represents a possible root) for Malay derivational morphology. We evaluate the validity of the affix patterns produced by our algorithm by comparing them with a list of affix patterns extracted from a hand-segmented list of derived words produced by a native speaker of Malay and an automatically derived list produced by a stemmer (Knowles and Mohd Don, 2006).

	Hand Segmented		Stemmer
	L_H-eval-news	L_H-eval-lit	L_S-eval-lit
Precision	33.17	27.14	40.7
Recall	61.11	58.06	36.16
F-Score	42.99	36.99	38.29
Lex. size	108	93	224
Pat. not recov.	42	39	143

Table 1: Experimental results

Error type	Analyzer Output	Hand-segment	Pattern error
Root-Pref.	meN-teR-nak	meN-ternak	meN-teR-X
Root-Suf.	beR-nila-i	beR-nilai	beR-X-i
Suffix Recursion	peN-tah-an-an	peN-tahan-an	X-an-an
All affix	peN-di-di-kan	peN-didik-an	peN-di-di-kan
OOV	beR-se-belah-an	-	ber-se-X-an

Table 2: Typical errors of affix patterns

3.5 Datasets

Four different corpora are used for training and evaluation. The first training corpus, used to build the morphology-based bigram model, consists of 14,869 word types compiled from Malay news articles. The pre-segmented list, *L-model-news*, contains 8,563 derived words (13,514 unique bigrams). The second corpus, used for EM training, consists of 18,438 word types collected from Malay literature. After post-processing, the pre-segmented list, *L-train-lit*, contains 15,916 derived words producing 215 unique affix patterns. For evaluation, two separate corpora are collected from Malay news articles and literature. The news articles contain 5,797 word types with 2,584 derived words (L_H*-eval-news*), producing 108 unique affix patterns, while the literature has 2,832 word types with 1,439 derived words (L_H*-eval-lit*), producing 93 unique affix patterns. Finally, we use a reference list of derivational history (L_S*-eval-lit*) collected by Knowles and Mohd Don (2006) from 4 Malay texts (119,471 words) and generated by a stemmer (224 affix patterns).

4 Results and Evaluation

To evaluate the lexicon we extracted from the training data, we compared the affix patterns extracted from the evaluation corpora, by hand or using the stemmer, with the patterns in the lexicon. The results are shown in Table 1.

There are a few observations to be made from these results. Firstly, our implementation of EM is still biased towards shorter morpheme sequences despite the added normalizing factor α, failing to choose correct segmentations with longer sequences. Secondly, a large amount of data is crucial to extract as many unique affix patterns as possible (an average of 4 unique affix patterns per 100 derived words). The limited amount of hand-segmented data used as the gold standard and the tendency of our algorithm to choose words with fewer morphemes represent major weaknesses in our evaluation, resulting in very low precision values (33.17% and 27.14%). Thirdly, the use of different domains for evaluation does not seem to affect the results, suggesting that domain is not a critical factor in collecting diversified affix patterns. Finally, we find that most affix patterns not recovered from the training corpus are either out of the vocabulary or result from ambiguous affixes that also exist as parts of roots (affix-like syllables). These ambiguous affixes occur so often that our algorithm fails to tell them apart. Table 2 shows typical errors produced by the analyzer.

5 Conclusion and Future Work

We have explored the feasibility of using a naïve morphological analyzer, a morphology-based language model, and EM training for learning the derivational morphology of an under-resourced language like Malay. As far as we know, this is the first attempt to combine these three methods in the learning of morphology. Our low precision and F-score indicate that our algorithm suffers from over-segmentation, which we believe is due to the small reference sets used for evaluation. Despite the discouraging overall results, our promising recall values (61.11% and 58.06%) show that most of the frequent affix patterns from our gold standard are recognized from the analysis. Eventually, the error analysis can serve as a guideline to improve the performance of the Malay morphological analyzer. In future, we will compare the performance of our algorithm with Morfessor 1.0 for unsupervised morphology learning (Creutz and Lagus, 2005). Our ultimate goal is to construct a hierarchical lexicon for Malay derivational morphology by clustering affixes based on their positions, precedence and lexical classes with the help of the improved analyzer.

Acknowledgments

The first author is funded by the Ministry of Higher Education of Malaysia.

References

Marco Baroni, Johannes Matiasek, and Harald Trost. 2002. Unsupervised discovery of morphologically related words based on orthographic and seman-tic similarity. In *Proceedings of the ACL Workshop on Morphological and Phonological Learning*, pages 48–57, Philadelphia, PA.

Kenneth Beesley and Lauri Karttunen. 2003. *Finite-State Morphology*. CSLI Publications.

Stanley Chen and Joshua Goodman. 1998. An empirical study of smoothing techniques for language modeling. Technical Report TR-10-98, Harvard University.

Mathias Creutz and Krista Lagus. 2005. Unsupervised morpheme segmentation and morphology induction from text corpora using morfessor 1.0. Technical Report A81, Publications in Computer and Information Science, Helsinki, Finland.

Arthur Dempster, Nan Laird, and Donald Rubin. 1977. Maximum likelihood from incomplete data via the EM algorithm. *Journal of the Royal Statistical Society*, Series B(34):1–38.

Eric Gaussier. 1999. Unsupervised learning of derivational morphology from inflectional lexicons. In *Proceedings of the ACL Workshop on Unsupervised Learning in Natural Language Processing*, pages 24–30, College Park, MD.

Xianping Ge, Wanda Prat, and Padhraic Smyth. 1999. Discovering Chinese words from unsegmented text. In *Proceedings of the 22nd Annual International ACM SIGIR Conference on Research and Development in Information Retrieval*, pages 271–272, Berkeley, CA.

John Goldsmith. 2001. Unsupervised learning of the morphology of a natural language. *Computational Linguistics*, 27(2):153–198.

Chunyu Kit, Zhiming Xu, and Jonathan Webster. 2003. Integrating $n$gram model and case-based learning for Chinese word segmentation. In *Proceedings of the Second SIGHAN Workshop on Chinese Language Processing*, pages 160–163, Sapporo, Japan.

Gerald Knowles and Zuraidah Mohd Don. 2006. *Word Class in Malay: A Corpus Based Approach*. Dewan Bahasa dan Pustaka, Kuala Lumpur, Malaysia.

Oskar Kohonen, Sami Virpioja, and Mikaela Klami. 2008. Allomorfessor: Towards unsupervised morpheme analysis. In *Proceedings of the 9th Cross-language Evaluation Forum Conference on Evaluating Systems for Multilingual and Multimodal Information Access*, pages 975–982, Aarhus, Denmark.

Fuchun Peng and Dale Schuurmans. 2001. Self-supervised Chinese word segmentation. In *Proceedings of the 4th International Conference on Advances in Intelligent Data Analysis*, pages 238–247, Cascais, Portugal.

Martha Y. Tachbelie. 2010. *Morphology-Based Language Modeling for Amharic*. Ph.D. thesis, University of Hamburg, Hamburg, Germany.

Punjabi Language Stemmer for nouns and proper names

Vishal Gupta
Assistant Professor, UIET
Panjab University Chandigarh
Vishal_gupta100@yahoo.co.in

Gurpreet Singh Lehal
Professor, Department of Computer Science,
Punjabi University Patiala
gslehal@yahoo.com

Abstract

This paper concentrates on Punjabi language noun and proper name stemming. The purpose of stemming is to obtain the stem or radix of those words which are not found in dictionary. If stemmed word is present in dictionary, then that is a genuine word, otherwise it may be proper name or some invalid word. In Punjabi language stemming for nouns and proper names, an attempt is made to obtain stem or radix of a Punjabi word and then stem or radix is checked against Punjabi noun and proper name dictionary. An in depth analysis of Punjabi news corpus was made and various possible noun suffixes were identified like ◌ੀਆਂ īāṃ, ◌ਿਆਂ iāṃ, ◌ੂਆਂ ūāṃ, ◌ਾਂ āṃ, ◌ੀਏ īē etc. and the various rules for noun and proper name stemming have been generated. Punjabi language stemmer for nouns and proper names is applied for Punjabi Text Summarization. The efficiency of Punjabi language noun and Proper name stemmer is 87.37%.

1 Introduction

stemming is the process for reducing inflected or sometimes derived words to their stem, base or root form, generally a written word form. The stem need not be identical to the morphological root of the word, it is usually sufficient that related words map to the same stem, even if this stem is not in itself a valid root. A stemmer for English, for example, should identify the string cats and possibly catlike, catty etc. as based on the root cat, and stemmer, stemming, stemmed as based on stem. A stemming algorithm reduces the words fishing, fished, fish, and fisher to the root word, fish. Stemming is an operation that conflates morphologically similar terms into a single term without doing complete morphological analysis. Stemming (Haidar et al., 2006) is used in information retrieval systems to improve performance. Additionally, this operation reduces the number of terms in the information retrieval system, thus decreasing the size of the index files.

In Punjabi language stemming (Mandeep et al.,2009) for nouns and proper names, an attempt is made to obtain stem or radix of a Punjabi word and then stem or radix is checked against Punjabi noun morph and proper names list. An in depth analysis of Punjabi news corpus was made and various possible noun suffixes were identified like ◌ੀਆਂ īāṃ, ◌ਿਆਂ iāṃ, ◌ੂਆਂ ūāṃ, ◌ਾਂ āṃ, ◌ੀਏ īē etc. and the various rules for noun and proper name stemming have been generated. Punjabi language stemmer for nouns and proper names is applied for Punjabi Text Summarization. Text Summarization is the process of condensing the source text into shorter version. Those sentences containing Punjabi language nouns or proper names are important.

2 Background and Related Work

The earliest English stemmer was developed by Julie Beth Lovins in 1968. The Porter stemming algorithm (Martin Porter, 1980), which was published later, is perhaps the most widely used algorithm for English stemming. Both of these stemmers are rule based and are best suited for less inflectional languages like English. (Goldsmith, 2001) proposed an algorithm for the morphology of a language based on the minimum description length (MDL) framework which focuses on representing the data in as compact manner as possible. (Creutz, 2005) uses probabilistic maximum a posteriori (MAP) formulation for morpheme segmentation.

Not much work has been reported for stemming for Indian languages compared to English and other European languages. The earliest work reported by (Ramanathan and Rao, 2003) used a hand crafted suffix list and performed longest match stripping for building a Hindi stemmer. (Majumder et al., 2007) developed statistical approach YASS: Yet Another Suffix Stripper which uses a clustering based approach based on string distance measures and requires no linguis-

Proceedings of the 2nd Workshop on South and Southeast Asian Natural Language Processing (WSSANLP), IJCNLP 2011, , pages 35–39,
Chiang Mai, Thailand, November 8, 2011.

tic knowledge. They concluded that stemming improves recall of IR systems for Indian languages like Bengali. (Dasgupta and Ng, 2007) worked on morphological parsing for Bengali. (Pandey and Siddiqui, 2008) proposed an unsupervised stemming algorithm for Hindi based on (Goldsmith, 2001) approach.

3 Punjabi Language stemmer for Nouns and Proper names

In Punjabi language stemming (Md. et al., 2007) for nouns and proper names, an attempt is made to obtain stem or radix of a Punjabi word and then stem or radix is checked against Punjabi noun morph and Proper names list. An in depth analysis of corpus was made and the possible noun and proper name suffixes (Praveen et al.,2003) were identified (Table1) and the various rules for Punjabi word noun stemming have been generated.

Table 1. Punjabi language noun/Proper name suffix list

◌ੀਆਂ īāṃ	◌ਿਆਂ iāṃ	◌ੂਆਂ ūāṃ	◌ਾਂ āṃ
◌ੀਏ īē	◌ੇ ē	◌ੀਓ Īō	◌ਿਓ iō
◌ੋ ō	◌ੀਆ īā	◌ਿਆ Iā	◌ੀਂ īṃ
ਈ ī	◌ੋਂ ōṃ	ਵਾਂ vāṃ	◌ਿਉਂ iuṃ
ਈਆ īā	ਜ/ਜ਼/ਸ ja/z/s		

Proper names are the names of person, place and concept etc. not occurring in Punjabi Dictionary. Proper Names play an important role in deciding a sentence's importance. From the Punjabi corpus, 17598 words have been identified as proper names. The percentage of these proper names words in the Punjabi corpus is about 13.84 %. Some of Punjabi language proper names are given in Table2.

Table 2. Some of Punjabi language proper names

ਅਕਾਲੀ akālī	ਲੁਧਿਆਣਾ ludhiāṇā
ਬਾਦਲ bādal	ਪਟਿਆਲਾ paṭiālā
ਜਲੰਧਰ jalndhar	ਭਾਜਪਾ bhājapā

Algorithm of Punjabi language stemmer for nouns and proper names is given below:

Stemming Algorithm

The algorithm of Punjabi language stemmer for nouns and proper names proceeds by segmenting the source Punjabi text into sentences and words. For each word of every sentence follow following steps:

- Step 1 : If current Punjabi word ends with ◌ੀਆਂ īāṃ then remove ਆਂ āṃ from end.
- Step 2 : Else If current Punjabi word ends with ◌ਿਆਂ iāṃ then remove ਆਂ āṃ from end.
- Step 3 : Else If current Punjabi word ends with ◌ੂਆਂ ūāṃ then remove ਆਂ āṃ from end.
- Step 4 : Else If current Punjabi word ends with ◌ੀਏ īē then remove ਏ ē from end.
- Step 5 : Else If current Punjabi word ends with ਈ ī then remove ਈ ī from end.
- Step 6 : Else If current Punjabi word ends with ◌ੇ ē then remove ◌ੇ ē from end and add kunna at the end
- Step 7 : Else If current Punjabi word ends with ◌ੀਓ Īō then remove ਓ ō from end.
- Step 8 : Else If current Punjabi word ends with ◌ਿਓ iō then remove ◌ਿਓ iō from end and add kunna at the end
- Step 9 : Else If current Punjabi word ends with ਵਾਂ vāṃ then remove ਵਾਂ vāṃ from end.
- Step 10 : Else If current Punjabi word ends with ◌ਾਂ āṃ then remove ◌ਾਂ āṃ from end.
- Step 11 : Else If current Punjabi word ends with ◌ੋਂ ōṃ then remove ◌ੋਂ ōṃ from end.
- Step 12 : Else If current Punjabi word ends with ◌ੋ ō then remove ◌ੋ ō from end and add kunna at the end
- Step 13 : Else If current Punjabi word ends with ◌ੀਂ īṃ then remove ◌ੀਂ īṃ from end.
- Step 14 : Else If current Punjabi word ends with ◌ਿਉਂ iuṃ then remove ◌ਿਉਂ iuṃ from end and add kunna at the end.

- Step 15: Else If current Punjabi word ends with ੀਆ ā then remove ਆ ā from end.
- Step 16: Else If current Punjabi word ends with ਿਆ ā then remove ਿਆ ā from end and add kunna at the end.
- Step 17: Else If current Punjabi word ends with ਈਆ īā then remove ਆ ā from end.
- Step 18: Else If current Punjabi word ends with ਜ/ਜ਼/ਸ ja/z/s then remove ਜ/ਜ਼/ਸ ja/z/s from end.
- Step 19: Current Punjabi Stemmed word is checked against Punjabi noun morph or Proper names list. If found, It is Punjabi noun or Punjabi Proper name.

Algorithm Input: ਫੁੱਲਾਂ phullāṃ (Flowers) and ਲੜਕੀਆਂ laṛkīāṃ (Girls)

Algorithm Output: ਫੁੱਲ phull (Flower) and ਲੜਕੀ laṛkī (Girl)

Some results of Punjabi language stemmer for nouns and Proper names for various possible suffixes are given in table3.

Table3.Results of Punjabi language Noun/Proper name stemmer

Punjabi Noun/Proper Name word	Stem word	suffix
ਕਸਾਈਆ Kasāīā	ਕਸਾਈ kasāī	ਈਆ īā
ਫਿਰੋਜ਼ਪੁਰੋਂ phirōzpurōṃ	ਫਿਰੋਜ਼ਪੁਰ phirōzpur	ੋਂ ōṃ
ਲੜਕੀਆਂ laṛkīāṃ	ਲੜਕੀ laṛkī	ੀਆਂ īāṃ
ਫੁੱਲਾਂ phullāṃ	ਫੁੱਲ phull	ਾਂ āṃ
ਲੜਕਿਆਂ laṛkiāṃ	ਲੜਕਾ laṛkā	ਿਆਂ iāṃ
ਮੁੰਡੇ muṇḍē	ਮੁੰਡਾ muṇḍā	ੇ ē
ਲੜਕਿਓ laṛkīō	ਲੜਕਾ laṛkā	ਿਓ iō
ਘਰੀਂ gharīṃ	ਘਰ ghar	ੀਂ īṃ
ਪਰਾਂਦੇ parāndc̄	ਪਰਾਂਦਾ parāndā	ੇ c̄
ਮਾਹੀਆ māhīā	ਮਾਹੀ Māhī	ੀਆ Īā
ਭਾਸ਼ਾਵਾਂ bhāshāvāṃ	ਭਾਸ਼ਾ bhāshā	ਵਾਂ vāṃ
ਆਗੂਆਂ āgūāṃ	ਆਗੂ āgū	ੂਆਂ ūāṃ
ਲੜਕੋ laṛkō	ਲੜਕਾ laṛkā	ੋ ō
ਲੜਕੀਏ laṛkīē	ਲੜਕੀ laṛkī	ੀਏ īē
ਲੜਕੀਓ laṛkīō	ਲੜਕੀ laṛkī	ੀਓ Īō
ਲੜਕਿਆ laṛkiā	ਲੜਕਾ laṛkā	ਿਆ iā
ਮੋਗਿਉਂ mōgiuṃ	ਮੋਗਾ mōgā	ਿਉਂ iuṃ
ਭਾਸ਼ਾਈ bhāshāī	ਭਾਸ਼ਾ bhāshā	ਈ Ī
ਸਟੂਡੈਂਟਸ saṭūḍaiṇṭas	ਸਟੂਡੈਂਟ saṭūḍaiṇṭa	ਸ s

4 Results and Discussions

An In depth analysis of output of Punjabi language stemmer for nouns and proper names has been done over 50 Punjabi documents of Punjabi news corpus of 11.29 million words. The efficiency of Punjabi language noun and Proper name stemmer is 87.37%, which is tested over 50 Punjabi news documents of corpus and is ratio of actual correct results to total produced results by stemmer. Table4 gives accuracy percentage of various rules of stemmer which is ratio of correct results to total results produced under that rule, tested over 50 news documents. Table5 gives the error percentage analysis of various rules of Punjabi language stemmer. Errors are due to rules violation or dictionary errors or due to syntax mistakes. Dictionary errors are those errors in which, after stemming, stem word is not present in noun morph or Proper names list, but actually it is noun. Syntax errors are those errors, in which input Punjabi word is having some syntax mistake, but actually that word falls under any of stemming rules. Overall error percentage, due to rules violation is 9.78%, due to dictionary mistakes is 2.4% and due to spelling mistakes is

0.45%. Some of rules have not been taken in these table as we have not detected any accurate or in accurate words for those rules in the input Punjabi text.

Table 4. Accuracy %age analysis of rules of Punjabi stemmer for Nouns and Proper names

Punjabi Noun Suffix Rules	Accuracy Percentage of Correct words detected
Rule1 ੀਆਂ īāṃ	86.81%
Rule2 ਿਆਂ iāṃ	95.91%
Rule3 ੂਆਂ ūāṃ	94.44%
Rule4 ਾਂ āṃ	92.55%
Rule5 ੇ ē	57.43%
Rule6 ੀਂ īṃ	100%
Rule7 ੋਂ ōṃ	100%
Rule8 ਵਾਂ vāṃ	79.16%

Table 5. Error %age analysis of various rules of Punjabi stemmer for nouns and proper names

Punjabi Noun Suffix Rules	% age of In Correct words due to rules Violation	% age of In Correct words due to dictionary mistakes	% age of In Correct words due to spelling mistakes
Rule1 ੀਆਂ īāṃ	79.7%	20.30%	0%
Rule2 ਿਆਂ iāṃ	86.65%	13.35%	0%
Rule3 ੂਆਂ ūāṃ	0%	100%	0%
Rule4 ਾਂ āṃ	68.71%	18.25%	13.04%
Rule5 ੇ ē	82.21%	17.79%	0%
Rule6 ੀਂ īṃ	0%	0%	0%
Rule7 ੋਂ ōṃ	0%	0%	0%
Rule8 ਵਾਂ vāṃ	89%	11%	0%

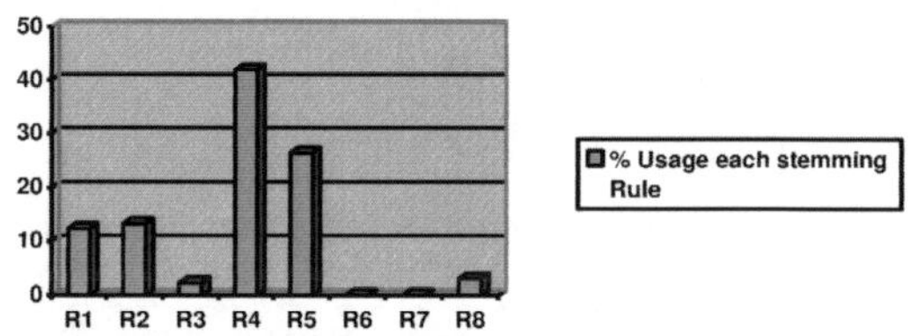

Graph 1 Percentage Frequency of Various Stemming Rules

Graph1 depicts the percentage usage of the stemming rules. As can be seen, Rule 4 and Rule 5 are the most frequently used stemming rules. Unfortunately Rule 5 has a low accuracy with 42.57% of words being wrongly stemmed by this rule. Actually some of Punjabi words like ਹੱਸੇ hassē (laugh), ਹਲਕੇ halkē (area), ਮੌਕੇ moukē (oppurtinity) and ਬਦਲੇ badlē (revenge) are not nouns and are not present in noun morph, but they fall under Rule5 of stemmer which makes them noun after stemming, which is not true.If after stemming, root word is still not present in dictionary then, that word may be a proper name or may be syntactically wrong word which can be ignored.

4 Conclusions

In this paper, we have discussed the Punjabi language stemmer for nouns and proper names. Most of the lexical resources used such as Punjabi proper names list, Punjabi noun morph etc. had to be developed from scratch as no work had been done in that direction. For developing these resources an in depth analysis of Punjabi corpus, Punjabi dictionary (Gurmukh et al.,1999) and Punjabi morph had to be carried out using manual and automatic tools. This the first time some of these resources have been developed for Punjabi and they can be beneficial for developing other Natural Language Processing applications in Punjabi. Punjabi language stemmer for nouns and proper names is successfully used in Punjabi language Text Summarization.

References

Creutz, Mathis, and Krista Lagus. 2005. *Unsu pervised morpheme segmentation and mor phology induction from text corpora using Mor fessor 1.0.* Technical Report A81, Publications in Computer and Information Science, Helsinki University of Technology.

Dasgupta, Sajib, and Vincent Ng. 2006. *Unsupervised Morphological Parsing of Bengali*. Language Resources and Evaluation, 40(3-4):311-330.

Haidar Harmani, Walid Keirouz, & Saeed Raheel. 2006. *A rule base extensible stemmer for Informa tion retrieval with application to Arabic*, The international Arab journal of information technol ogy, Vol No.3, Issue No.3, pp 265-272.

Goldsmith, John A. 2001.*learning of the morphology of a natural language*, Computational Linguistics, 27(2):153-198.

Gurmukh Singh, Mukhtiar Singh Gill and S.S. Joshi. 1999. *Punjabi to English Bilingual Dictionary.* Punjabi University Patiala.

Majumder, Prasenjit, Mandar Mitra, Swapan K. Parui, Gobinda Kole, Pabitra Mitra, and Kalyankumar Datta. 2007. *YASS: Yet another suffix stripper.* Association for Computing Machinery Transac tions on Information Systems, 25(4):18-38.

Mandeep Singh Gill, G.S. Lehal and S.S. Joshi. 2009. *Part of Speech Tagging for Grammar Checking of Punjabi.* The Linguistic Journal Volume 4 Issue 1, 6-21.

Md. Zahurul Islam, Md. Nizam Uddin and Mumit Khan. 2007. *A light weight stemmer for Bengali and its Use in spelling Checker.* Proc. 1st Intl. Conf. on Digital Comm. and Computer Applica tions (DCCA07), Irbid, Jordan, March 19-23.

Pandey, Amaresh K., and Tanveer J. Siddiqui. 2008. An unsupervised Hindi stemmer with heuristic improvements. In Proceedings of the Second Workshop on Analytics For Noisy Unstructured Text Data, 303:99-105.

Porter, Martin F. 1980. *An algorithm for suffix strip ping Program*, 14(3):130-137.

Praveen Kumar, Shrikant Kashyap, Ankush Mittal and Sumit Gupta. 2003. *A query answering system for E learning Hindi documents.* South Asian Language Review, VOL.XIII, Nos 1&2.

Ramanathan, Ananthakrishnan, and Durgesh D. Rao. 2003. *A Lightweight Stemmer for Hindi*, Workshop on Computational Linguistics for South-Asian Lan guages, EACL.

Challenges in Urdu Text Tokenization and Sentence Boundary Disambiguation

Zobia Rehman, Waqas Anwar, Usama Ijaz Bajwa
Department of Computer Science
COMSATS Institute of Information Technology, Abbottabad, Pakistan
{zobiarehman,waqas,usama}@ciit.net.pk

Abstract

Urdu is morphologically rich language with different nature of its characters. Urdu text tokenization and sentence boundary disambiguation is difficult as compared to the language like English. Major hurdle for tokenization is improper use of space between words, where as absence of case discrimination makes the sentence boundary detection a difficult task. In this paper some issues regarding both of these language processing tasks have been identified.

1 Introduction

Urdu is morphologically rich language, spoken by more than 150 million people of the world; either as their mother tongue or as their second language. This language is composed of many different languages, e.g. Arabic, Persian, Turkish, Hindi, Sanskrit, and English. Moreover it adopts new words from other languages. It is a bidirectional language and uses Arabic based orthography. Morphology of Urdu language is influenced by all the languages mentioned above (Riaz, 2007) (Waqas et al., 2006).

Text tokenization is the process of identifying word peripheries in written text. It divides the text into its constituent words (Kaplan, 2005) (Manning et al., 1999). It is a preliminary task for all language processing systems, e.g., machine translation, part of speech tagging, information retrieval, information extraction, grammar checker, and spell checker. All these language processing systems need their input text with definite word boundaries.

Sentence boundary disambiguation is the process of identifying sentence terminating punctuations in written text. It divides the text into its component sentences. Sentence boundary has its own importance in above mentioned language processing systems as well as it is equally important for; text summarization, text paragraphing, parsing, and chunking. These systems need their input text properly alienated into sentences. Tokenization and sentence boundary disambiguation are not easy tasks for Urdu language. Urdu is a complex language with respect to its morphology and nature of its characters. In hand written Urdu text there is no convention to use space for the isolation of words from one another. The native speaker of the language decides about the word boundary by just looking at the shape of characters. Tokenization becomes easy, if there is use of space between words but in the computer typed Urdu text the use of space is extremely uneven; as it is used in some specific situations and this conditional use of spaces makes tokenization even more complex (Lehal, 2010). English also has another advantage of case discrimination in characters. This case discrimination is helpful in identifying sentence boundaries. But Urdu also lacks the case discrimination, which is the only hint to know the starting point of a sentence.

2 Literature review

2.1 Segmentation techniques

Numerous tokenization techniques are used for various languages of the world, e.g., rule based techniques (Kaplan, 2005) , statistical techniques (Lehal, 2010) , fuzzy techniques (Shahabi et al, 2007), lexical techniques (Wu et al., 1994) (Xing et al., 2008) , and feature based techniques (Meknavin, 1997). Significant work has been done for Arabic (Attia, 2007) and Persian language (Shamsford et al., 2009) also. In (Lehal, 2010) Space omission issues of Urdu script have been addressed and resolved using bilingual corpora and statistical word disambiguation techniques.

Proceedings of the 2nd Workshop on South and Southeast Asian Natural Language Processing (WSSANLP), IJCNLP 2011, , pages 40–45,
Chiang Mai, Thailand, November 8, 2011.

2.2 Techniques for sentence boundary detection

The task of sentence boundary disambiguation is performed for numerous languages. Although few of them are Arabic script languages, written from right to left, but still no significant work has been done for Urdu sentence boundary disambiguation.
Various techniques have been used for different languages, e.g., rule based techniques (Dincer et al., 2004), collocation identification (Kiss et al., 2006), regular expressions (Walker et al., 2001), finite state models (Rezaei, 2001), heuristic rules, artificial neural network models (Palmer et al., 1994) and part of speech tagging (Mikheev, 2000).

3 Issues of text tokenization in Urdu

There is no concept of the space in hand written Urdu text. A native speaker of this language can understand and identify where a word ends and from where a new word starts. But a machine can not behave like a native speaker of the language and can not interpret a text without obvious boundaries of words. If there are two words "آبی" (water) and "پرندے" (birds), in hand written text a speaker can distinguish between the two words but if these two words are written in any computer application then they must be separated with space so that machine can understand them as two different words, e.g., "آبی پرندے" (water birds). To avoid space character, a unique Urdu character known as Zero Width Non-Joiner is used. It just separates the two words without any space between them, e.g., "آبی‌پرندے" (water birds). If space or zero width non joiner are not used then it will consider them a single word, e.g., "آبیپرندے" (water birds), which is not understandable even for the native speaker of the language.

There are two types of characters in Urdu; Joiner and non joiner characters. Inter word space is only used when a word ends with a joiner character. If the word ends with a non joiner character then this space is rarely used. So to properly tokenize the Urdu text, it is needed to manipulate space between words.

Tokenization issues can be mainly divided into following two categories;

- Space inclusion issues
- Space exclusion issues

3.1 Space inclusion issues

When words are written in a way without space between them, then it is needed to insert space between them, so that machine can understand their boundaries. There are many languages in the world, in which words are written without any space. This issue is not easy to resolve as there are numerous ways to insert space between the words. Moreover every way conveys different context of the text.
In Urdu, space insertion is needed in following two cases:

- When word ends with non joiner character.
- When zero width non joiner (ZWNJ) is used between two words.

3.1.1 Word ending at non joiner

Characters given in following table are known as non joiner or separator characters in Urdu.

ا د ڈ ذ ر ز ڑ ژ و ے

Table 1. Non joiner characters in Urdu

These characters have the specialty that they can only acquire final shape and can not adopt initial or medial shapes. Any joiner character can be attached at their start but they can not be attached at the start of the joiner character. When a word ends with such a non joiner then space is not inserted after it, as for a native speaker there will be no ambiguity to distinguish it from other words (Naim, 1999) (Siddiqi, 1971). Consult Table 2. for such examples

اسدشہرسےباہرجاپہنچا (I)	اسد شہر سے باہر جا پہنچا (II)
Asad reached out of the city.	

Table 2. Words ending at non joiners

In example (I) words are written without inter word space and in (II) words are written with space at the end of each word. It is obvious that all the words end at non joiner that's why in examples, I and II the sentence gives the same meanings. Native speaker can understand that both of the examples have same words but example (I) is considered by machine as a single vague word.

It is a major issue how to tokenize a string if it has more than one possible combination. Native speaker can identify the discrete words in this case also by looking at surrounding words but for machine it is impossible.

3.1.2 Use of ZWNJ between two words

Zero width non joiner is used between two words when it is needed to separate them from each other. But ZWNJ does not help to distinguish between word boundaries. It just helps to separate them visually. For example "پرانی‌سڑک" (old track), in it both words are separated by an additional ZWNJ character.

(old track) پرانیسڑک (Words without space or ZWNJ)
(old track) پرانی سڑک (Words separated by space)
(old track) پرانی‌سڑک (Words separated by ZWNJ)

Table 3. ZWNJ between words

Tokenizer is also responsible to remove this ZWNJ and insert space instead of it so words can be literally separated.

3.2 Space exclusion issues

Space exclusion is another issue of text tokenization. The space that is used to separate the words, some times occurs between words, collectively giving the single meaning. During tokenization these words need to be assigned single boundary. Therefore the space between such words is needed to be excluded.

In following cases this space should be neglected while assigning boundaries to words:

- Compound words
- Reduplication
- Affixation
- Proper nouns
- English words
- Abbreviations and Acronyms

3.2.1 Compound words

In Urdu there are following categories of compound words with respect to their formation (Sproat, 1992) (Schmidt, 1999) (Javed, 1985):

- AB formation
- A-o-B formation
- A-e-B formation

It is needed to treat them as a single word as these different combinations form a single word.

3.2.1.1 AB formation

In AB formation two roots or stems join together to form a semantically single word. When first word in the compound unit, ends with a non joiner then it is rare to have a space between them, e.g., "کھاتاپیتا" (well-off) but if it ends with a joiner then space is inserted after it. During tokenization this space must be neglected and these words should be assigned a single boundary (Sproat, 1992). See Table 2. for such examples

(hard work) محنت مشقت
(basic needs of life) روٹی کپڑا
(parents) ماں باپ

Table 4. AB formation of compound words

3.2.1.2 A-o-B formation

In A-o-B formation two roots or stems are linked to each other with the help of a linking morpheme 'و' and make a single semantic unit. If the first morpheme ends at a non joiner then there is no need to insert space between it and linking morpheme, e.g., "درودیوار" (boundary). But if the first morpheme ends with joiner then space is used between it and the linking morpheme. So the tokenizer must neglect this space and consider the compound unit as a single token (Sproat, 1992).
Consider the following examples in Table 5. In it space is used before and after the linking morpheme. Without the space these words will not be understandable even for the native speaker but use of the space brings hurdle, if it is needed to assign a single boundary to these words.

(honor) عزت و حرمت
(discipline) نظم و ضبط
(law and order) امن و امان

Table 5. A-o-B formation of compound words

3.2.1.3 A-e-B formation

In A-e-B formation "e" is the linking morpheme which shows the relation between A and B. morpheme "e" is represented in Urdu by diacritic "ِ". But before tokenization all diacritics are removed and "ِ" is replaced by space (Sproat, 1992). See the examples in Table 6.

(prime minister) وزیر اعظم
(student) طالب علم
(scene limit) حد نظر

Table 6. A-e-B formation of compound words

Words of this type must be assigned a single word boundary by excluding the inter word space between them.

3.2.2 Reduplication

Reduplicated words must also be considered a single semantic unit and if there is a space between them, then it should be excluded in order to assign a single boundary to reduplicated words (Sproat, 1992).

دن بدن (day by day)	دھوم دھام (pomp & show)	اٹھ اٹھ (getup)
حرف بحرف (character by character)	صبح صبح (early morning)	روٹی ووٹی (bread)

Table 7. Reduplication of words

In the examples in Table 7, all the reduplicated words are separated by space. Tokenizer is responsible to neglect this space and mark them as a single word.

3.2.3 Affixation

Affixes are commonly used in Urdu. Both prefixes and suffixes are used in it. Whenever any affix (prefix or suffix) or stem are individual morphemes and prefix ends with a joiner then space is inserted between the prefix and the stem. Similarly if the stem ends with a joiner then space is inserted between stem and suffix. But they are single semantic units so these must be encapsulated in a single boundary by excluding the space between stem and affix (Sproat, 1992) (Platts, 2002). See the examples of prefixes in Table 8.

خوش اخلاق (polite)	خوش نصیب (lucky)
بیش قیمت (expensive)	ان تھک (hard work)

Table 8. Prefixation

See the examples of suffixes given in Table 9.

آلہ کار (apparatus)	حیرت انگیز (amazing)
سرمایہ کاری (investment)	شادی شدہ (married)
غلط فہمی (misunderstanding)	دہشت ناک (fearful)

Table 9. Suffixation

3.2.4 Proper nouns

Most of the time proper names are divided into first name and last name or into first name,second name and last name (Schmidt, 1999). It is often seen that space is used between these parts but this space should be excluded, so that a name with all its parts can become a single token (Sproat, 1992). Proper noun examples are given in Table 10.

سعودی عرب (Saudi Arabia)	حسن علی (Hassan Ali)
اسلام آباد (Islamabad)	صالح بانو (Sawliha Bano)
جنوبی افریقہ (South Africa)	زینب نور (Zainab Noor)

Table 10. Proper nouns containing more than one constituent

3.2.5 English words

Some of the English words are used in Urdu. These words are often composed of more than one morpheme. When first of these morphemes, written in Urdu ends with a joiner character then space is used between them. This space should be neglected by the tokenizer to assign these words a single boundary (Sproat, 1992). Such examples are given in Table 11.

ٹیلی کمیونیکیشن (telecommunication)	ٹیسٹ میچ (test match)
نیٹ ورک (network)	میڈیکل سنٹر (medical center)
فٹ بال (football)	ایش ٹرے (ash tray)

Table 11. Words of English language commonly used in Urdu

3.2.6 Abbreviations and acronyms

English abbreviations are used in Urdu, in the form of pronunciation of English characters, written in Urdu, with space between each character's pronunciations. These abbreviations behave as a single word. If these are followed by any name then along with the name they form a single unit (Sproat, 1992). Abbreviation and acronym examples in Urdu are given in Table 12.

(M.Qureshi) ایم قریشی	(PhD) پی ایچ ڈی
(A.K. Shah) اے کے شاہ	(NLP) این ایل پی

Table 12. English abbreviations

4 Issues of Urdu sentence boundary disambiguation

According to linguists a sentence is an expression. It is a collection of words that conveys a complete thought and contains a subject and predicate. Subject is usually a single word or several words; noun or pronoun. It tells about what or whom the sentence is concerned. Predicate is a verb; it tells what the subject is doing or being in the sentence. In the simple most Urdu sentence the subject comes first, then predicate and finally the verb; whereas the object and the predicative nouns come in the middle of the sentence (Platts, 2002).

In Urdu language sentence boundary disambiguation, challenges arise due to its certain properties such as: absence of capitalization and the use of punctuation marks in abbreviations and acronyms. In English, characters can be written in upper and lower case and the difference in characters case is helpful in identifying the sentence boundaries. There is a convention in English language that if a period is followed by a word starting with capital letter then it has maximum probability to become a sentence marker. But in Urdu there are no case discriminations to indicate the start of the sentence

Punctuations like '-', '.', '؟' and '!' are used as sentence terminators and these can also be used inside the sentence; e.g., in Urdu text '-' is used to describe range between two values, in dates, part of abbreviation, and also as the line breaker. Examples for such cases are given in Table 13.

احمد پانچ – چه سال شہر سے باہر رہا- روزگار کے حصول کے لیے اسے دوردراز کے علاقوں کا سفر کرنا پڑا- (Ahmad was out of the city for five to six years. For the sake of job he had to travel far and wide.)
۲۰۰۵-۱۰-۰۸ کی صبح پاکستان میں زلزلے کے شدید جھٹکے محسوس ہوئے - On 08-10-2005, sever earthquake jolts had been felt in Pakistan.
یو- ایس- اے- کی معیشت پچھلےدو سالوں میں بہت ىبــر طرح متاثر ہوئ - The economy of the U.S.A. has been badly affected since previous two years.

Table 13. Use of (-) at different locations in an Urdu sentence

Full stop or '.' is also used as sentence terminator in Urdu script as well as the decimal symbol as shown in Table 14.

ریکٹرسکیل پہ زلزلے کی شدت ۸. ۷ ریکاڈ کی گیی. Intensity of the earthquake was 7.8 on Richter scale.

Table 14. Use of (.) at different locations

If there is punctuation inside the Urdu text then by just considering the characters of its surrounding words, it can not be decided that either a given punctuation is sentence terminator or not. Consult table 15. for such examples

واہ! کیا کمال کی جگہ هے- Wow! What a wonderful place.)
وہ چلایا،" میری مدد کرو-" (He Screamed, "Help me.")
کیوں؟ اس نے ایسی کیا غلطی کر دی؟ (Why? What did he do wrong?)

Table 15. Ambiguity in sentence boundary due to punctuations

Obviously in the above cases it is difficult for the machine to isolate the punctuations from sentence termination behavior.

5 Conclusion and Future work

In this paper issues are described for Urdu text tokenization and sentence boundary disambiguation. In hand written Urdu text, words are written in continuation without any space between them. But computer text files demand a separator, whenever a word ends with joiner character. Without any separator, word of this sort will join itself to next word resulting into an indefinite word that is not understandable even for the native speaker of the language. Demand of this separator is satisfied by inserting space character or zero width non joiner after the words ending with joiner characters. On the other hand words ending at non joiners are not followed by any space character or zero width non joiner. In short this intricate job is concerned to manipulate spaces between words, so that machine can demarcate their boundaries. Different statistical and rule based techniques have been applied on the different languages of the word, which are even much more complex than Urdu language, to solve their segmentation issues. In future we will target some of these techniques along with hand crafted dictionaries of Urdu compound words, affixations and some commonly used English words in Urdu script.

Sentence boundary disambiguation has its own challenges for Urdu. This task is easier to some extent in the languages with upper and lower case character discrimination. As in English there is convention that a period followed by a word starting with an upper case letter, has maximum probability to be a boundary marker. But in Urdu, the language without case discrimination, it is difficult to find the punctuations showing the behavior of sentence boundary. In future we are aimed to solve these issues by using part of speech information of each word followed by any putative sentence boundary. This information can be helpful to know that either the current word should be followed by a sentence terminator or not.

References

Attia, M. A. 2007. *Arabic tokenization system*, Proceedings of the 2007 Workshop on Computational Approaches to Semitic Language, 65 – 72.

Dincer B. and Karaoglan B. 2004. *Sentence Boundary Detection in Turkish*, *Advances in Information Systems*, Springer Berlin, pp. 255-262.

Javed I. 1985. *New Urdu Grammar.* Advance Urdu Buru New Dehali.

Kaplan. 2005. *Method of Tokenizing Text, Inquiries into Words, Constraints And Contexts.*

Kiss T. and Strunk J. 2006. *Unsupervised Multilingual Sentence Boundary Detection*, MIT press, Volume, 32, pp. 485-525.

Lehal G. 2010. *A word segmentation system for handling space omission problem in Urdu script,* WSSANLP, pp. 43-50.

Manning C. Schuetze H. 1999. *Foundations of Statistical Natural Language Processing.* MIT Press Massachusetts.

Meknavin, S. 1997.*Feature-based Thai Word Segmentation*, Proceedings of Natural Language Processing Pacific Rim Symposium, pp. 35 – 46.

Mikheev A. 2000. *Tagging Sentence Boundaries*, Proceedings of the 1st North American chapter of the Association for Computational Linguistics conference, vol 4, pp. 264-271.

Naim C. 1999. *Introductory Urdu.* South Asian Language & Area Center University of Chicago.

Palmer D. and Hearst M. 1994. *Adaptive Sentence Boundary Disambiguation*, Proceedings of the fourth conference on Applied natural language processing, Stuttgart, Germany, pp. 73-83.

Platts, J. 2002. *A Grammar of the Hindustani or Urdu Language*, Sang-e-Meel Publications, Lahore

Rezaei S. 2001. *Tokenizing an Arabic Script Language, Arabic NLP Workshop at ACL/EACL*, Toulouse, France.

Riaz K. 2007. *Challenges in Urdu stemming- a progress report*, BCS IRSG Symposium.

Ruth L. Schmidt. 1999. *Urdu, An Essential Grammar*, London: Routeledge Taylor & Francis Group.

Shahabi, A. S., Kangaveri, M.R. 2007. *Intelligent processing system*, IFIP International Federation of Information Processing, Springer Boston 2007, Vol. 228/2007, pp. 411- 420

Shamsford, M., Kiani,S., Shahidi,Y. 2009. *STeP-1: Standard text preparation for Persian language*, CAASL3 Third Workshop on Computational Approaches to Arabic Script- Languages.

Siddiqi. 1971. جامع القواعد. Markazi Urdu Board

Sproat, R. 1992. *Morphology and Computation.* The MIT Press.

Walker et al. 2001. *Sentence Boundary Detection: A Comparison of Paradigms for Improving MT Quality*, Machine translation in the information age", pp. 369-372.

Wu, D., Fung, P. 1994. *Improving Chinese Tokenization with Linguistic Filters on Statistical Lexical Acquisition*, Proceedings of the fourth conference on Applied natural language processing, pp. 180 – 181

Waqas A., Xuan W., Lu Li, Xiao-long W. 2006. A Survey of Automatic Urdu Language Processing. International Conference on Machine Learning and Cybernetics, pp: 4489-4494

Xing, H. C., Zhang, X., Dalians, H. 2008. *Using parallel corpora and Uplug to create a Chinease-English dictionary*, Thesis from Royal Institute of Technology.

Challenges in Developing a Rule based Urdu Stemmer

Sajjad Ahmad Khan, Waqas Anwar, Usama Ijaz Bajwa
Department of Computer Science
COMSATS Institute of Information Technology, Abbottabad, Pakistan
sajjadkhan25@hotmail.com,waqas@ciit.net.pk,usama@ciit.net.pk

Abstract

Urdu language raises several challenges to Natural Language Processing (NLP) largely due to its rich morphology. In this language, morphological processing becomes particularly important for Information Retrieval (IR). The core tool of IR is a Stemmer which reduces a word to its stem form. Due to the diverse nature of Urdu, developing stemmer is a challenging task. In Urdu, there are large numbers of variant forms (derivational and inflectional forms) for a single word form. The aim of this paper is to present issues pertaining to the development of Urdu stemmer (rule based stemmer).

1. Introduction

Urdu is an Indo-Aryan language. It is the national language of Pakistan and is one of the twenty-three official languages of India. It is written in Perso-Arabic script. The Urdu vocabulary consists of several languages including Arabic, English, Turkish, Sanskrit and Farsi (Persian) etc.
Urdu's script is right-to-left and form of a word's character is context sensitive, means the form of a character is dissimilar in a word because of the position of that character in the word (beginning, centre, on the ending) (Waqas et al., 2006).
In Urdu language, morphological processing becomes particularly important for Information Retrieval (IR). Information retrieval system is used to ensure easy access to stored information. It also deals with saving, representation and organization of information objects. Modules of an IR system consist of a group of information objects, a group of requests and a method to decide which information items are most possibly helping to meet the requirements of the requests. Inside IR, the information data which is stored and receives search calls usually corresponds to the lists of identifiers recognized as key terms, keywords. One of the attempts to make the search engines more efficient in information retrieval is the use of stemmer. Stem is the base or root form of a word. Stemmer is an algorithm that reduces the word to their stem/root form e.g. tested, testing, pretest and tester have the stem "test". Similarly the Urdu stemmer should stem the words کم عقل (senseless), عقل مند (sensible), عقل مندی (sagacity) to Urdu stem word عقل (sense). Stemming is part of the complex process of taking out the words from text and turning them into index terms in an IR system. Indexing is the process of selecting keywords for representing a document.
The smallest units of word which cannot be decomposed further into smaller meaningful units are called Morphemes.[1] They are of two kinds: free morphemes and bound morphemes. Morphemes which exist freely (alone) are called free morphemes whereas bound morphemes are made as a result of combination with another morpheme. For instance "flower" is a free morpheme, while "s" is the example of a bound morpheme.

The study of internal structure of words is called Morphology.[2] Deriving new words from the existing ones is called derivational morphemes e.g. Honour, Honourable, Honourably. Examples in Urdu: The words چاہت (love), چاہتا (to love) and چہیتا (lovely) are the derivatives of word چاہ (love). Those morphemes that produce the grammatical formation of a word is called Inflectional morphemes e.g. Boys. Examples in Urdu: The words سخت تر (harder) and سخت ترین (hardest) are the inflected forms of word سخت (hard).

The stemmer is also applicable to other natural language processing applications needing morphological analysis for example spell checkers, word frequency count studies, word parsing etc. The rest of the paper is organized as follows: In section 2, different rule based stemming algorithms are discussed. Section 3 gives an introduction regarding orthographic features. In section 4, several issues pertaining to Urdu stemmer are

[1] http://www.ielanguages.com/linguist.html
[2] http://introling.ynada.com/session-6-types-of-morphemes

Proceedings of the 2nd Workshop on South and Southeast Asian Natural Language Processing (WSSANLP), IJCNLP 2011, , pages 46–51,
Chiang Mai, Thailand, November 8, 2011.

discussed in detail. Conclusion of the study and the future work is discussed in section 5.

2. Stemming Algorithms

There are four kinds of stemming approaches (Frakes, R.Baeza-Yates, 1992): table lookup, affix removal, successor variety and n-grams. Table lookup method is also known as brute force method, where every word and its respective stem are stored in table. The stemmer finds the stem of the input word in the respective stem table. This process is very fast, but it has severe disadvantage i.e. large memory space required for words and their stems and the difficulties in creating such tables. This kind of stemming algorithm might not be practical. The affix removal stemmer eliminates affixes from words leaving a stem. The successor variety stemmer is based on the determination of morpheme borders, i.e., it needs information from linguistics, and is more complex than affix removal stemmer. The N-grams stemmer is based on the detection of bigrams and trigrams.

The (J.B. Lovins, 1968) published the first English stemmer and used about 260 rules for stemming the English language. She suggested a stemmer consisting of two-phases. The first stage removes the maximum possible ending which matches one on a redefined suffix list. The spelling exceptions are covered in the 2nd stage.

The (M.F. Porter, 1980) developed the stemmer on the truncation of suffixes, by means of list of suffixes and some restrictions/conditions are placed to recognize the suffix to be detached and generating a valid stem. Porter Stemmer performs stemming process in five steps. The Inflectional suffixes are handled in the first step, derivational suffixes are handling through the next three steps and the final step is the recoding step. Porter simplified the Lovin's rules upto 60 rules.

Different stemmers have also been developed for Arabic language. The (S. Khoja and R. Garside, 1999) developed an Arabic stemmer called a superior root-based stemmer, developed by Khoja and Garside. This stemming algorithm truncates prefixes, suffixes and infixes and then uses patterns for matching to pull out the roots. The algorithm has to face many problems particularly with nouns. The (Thabet. N., 2004) created a stemmer, which performs on classical Arabic in Quran to produce stem. For each *Surah*, this stemmer generates list of words. These words are checked in stop word list, if they don't exist in this list then corresponding prefixes and suffixes are removed from these words.

The (Eiman Tamah Al-Shammari, Jessica Lin, 2008) proposed the Educated Text Stemmer (ETS). It is a simple, dictionary free and efficient stemmer that decreases stemming errors and has lesser storage and time required.

Bon was the first stemmer developed for Persian language (M. Tashakori, M. Meybodi & F. Oroumchian, 2003). Bon is an iterative longest matching stemmer. The iterative longest matching stemmer truncates the longest possible morpheme from a word according to a set of rules. This procedure is repeated until no more characters can be eliminated. The (A. Mokhtaripour and S. Jahanpour, 2006) proposed a Farsi stemmer that works without dictionary. This stemmer first removes the verb and noun suffixes from a word. After that it starts truncation of prefixes from that word.

Till date only one stemmer i.e. Assas-Band, developed for Urdu language (Q. Akram, A. Naseer and S. Hussain, 2009). This stemmer extracts the stem/root word of only Urdu words and not of borrowed words i.e. words from Arabic, Persian and English words. This algorithm removes the prefix and suffix from a word and returns the stem word. This stemmer does not handle words having infixes.

3. Orthographic Features of Urdu

According to (Malik M G Abbas et al., 2008), Urdu alphabet consists of 35 simple consonants, 15 aspired consonants, 10 vowels, 15 diacritical marks, 10 digits and other symbols.

3.1 Consonants

Consonants are divided into two groups:

a. Aspirated Consonants

There are 15 aspirated consonants in Urdu language. These consonants are shown by a grouping of a simple consonant to be aspirated. A special letter called Heh Doachashmee (ھ) is used to mark the aspiration. Aspired Consonants are بھ، ڑھ، رھ، گھ، کھ، ڈھ، دھ، چھ، جھ، ٹھ، تھ، پھ، لھ، نھ، مھ

b. Non Aspirated Consonants

Urdu language consists of 35 non aspirated consonant signs that represent 27 consonant sounds. Various scripts are employed to show the similar sound in Urdu, For example: Sad (ص), Seen (س) and Seh (ث) represent the sound [s].

3.2 Vowels

Urdu has ten vowels. Seven of them contain nasalized forms. Out of these seven, four long vowels are represented by Alef Madda (آ), Alef (ا), Choti Yeh (ی) and Vav (و) and three short vowels are represented by Arabic Kasra (Zer), Arabic Fatha (Zabar) and Arabic Damma (Pesh). In Urdu language, the Vowel demonstration is context sensitive. For example, the Urdu Choti Yeh (ی) and Vav (و) can also be used as a consonant (Malik M G Abbas et al., 2008).

3.3 Aerab Marks

The aerab marks are those marks that are added to a letter to change the pronunciation of a word or to differentiate among similar words. It is also called as diacritical mark or diacritic.[3]
There are 15 accent marks in Urdu (Malik M G Abbas et al., 2008). Accent marks (Zabar, Zer, Pesh, Ulta Pesh, Do-Zabar, Do-Zer, Do-Pesh etc) represent vowel sounds. These are placed above or below of an Urdu word. The accent marks are very rarely used by people in writing Urdu. When the diacritic of a character in a word is changed then it could entirely change its meaning. These accent marks play a significant role in the right pronunciation and recognition of meaning of a sentence, such as:

درخت پر انگور کی بیل ہے۔
(A vine is on the tree)

and بیل گھاس کھا رہا ہے۔
(The bull is eating grass)

In the first sentence, the word (بیل) means "a creeping plant" or a "vine" while in the second sentence it means a "bull". To remove the doubt between these two words, there should be Zabar after Beh (ب) in the second sentence.

3.4 Special Characters

There are two special characters used in Urdu which are discussed bellow:

a. Hamza (ء)

Hamza is used to separate two consecutive vowels sounds. For example, in آوٴ (come), Hamza is separating two vowel sounds i.e. Alef Madda (آ) and Vav (و).

b. Heh Doachashmee (ھ)

Heh Doachashmee (ھ) changes the action of a simple consonant and makes it aspired consonant. For example, ج + ھ = جھ , پ + ھ = پھ
Examples in words: جھنڈا, پھل
(Flag, Fruit)

4. Issues in developing an Urdu Stemmer

4.1 Morphological rich language

Urdu is morphologically rich language. It produces high number of derivational and inflectional words for a single word form. There are 57 different forms that can be generated from a single Urdu word (Rizvi, S. & Hussain, M., 2005). For Example, some different forms of Urdu word پڑھ (read) are:

پڑھنا، پڑھا، پڑھے، پڑھیں، پڑھی، پڑھنی، پڑھو، پڑھوں،
پڑھا، پڑھانا، پڑھاتے، پڑھاتا، پڑھوا، پڑھواتا، پڑھوں

Besides its own vocabulary, the Urdu vocabulary also consists of large number of Arabic, Persian, Hindi and English words etc. Thus Urdu language inherits the characteristics of the above mentioned languages too and as a result stemming process becomes a challenging task. We cannot achieve a good level of precision if a stemmer of any borrowed language is used as a stemmer on Urdu words. The reason is that, the Arabic stemmer will just stem Arabic words that are used in Urdu as borrowed words and a Persian stemmer will just stem borrowed Persian words etc.
By using traditional process of modeling every form of a word as a unique word generates a lot of problems for Natural Language Processing applications such as growth of vocabulary, inflectional gaps, larger out-of-vocabulary rates and poor language model probability estimation.
The relation among words in Urdu is found by using inflecting nouns, postposition and pronouns to state case information, number and gender. Inflecting verbs to reproduce number, gender and person information etc. Inflecting adjectives are to agree with the noun in number, gender and case. Thus, the standard stemmers which are developed for English words are not practically implementable for Urdu language.

4.2 Engineering issues

Urdu is bidirectional language and electronically we cannot represent it in ASCII form. Such type of language is represented by a special character

[3] http://www.the-comma.com/diacritics.php

set called Unicode. The Arabic Orthography Unicode Standards are used to process Urdu.
Unicode is not supported by many programming languages. The languages that support Unicode include C#, Python and Java etc. Some programming language support Unicode but the IDE may not support it fully.

4.3 Diacritical Marks

Special attention should be given to the diacritical marks while developing an Urdu stemmer. The stem of an Urdu word changes with the use of these marks. For example عالم is used in two senses, when Zabar is placed above the character ع and on ل, then its meaning is *people* and its stem is عالم (people). But when Zer is placed below ل, then its meaning is *scholar* and its stem is علم (knowledge).
Similarly رسل word has two meanings. One is *messengers* when Pesh is used on ر and س with stem رسول (messenger) and other is *access* when Zabar is used on ر and س with stem ارسال (sending). Another example is the word خاتم , which has two meanings (The last/ring), the first one has stem ختم (finish) and second has خاتم (ring).

4.4 Compound Words

For word formation, compounding is one of the morphological procedures. The grouping of two words which already exist is called a compound word (Payne, Thomas E., 2006). When two or more than two lexeme stems are merged together to produce another lexeme, then it is called compound word (Sproat. R., 1992). Examples are: Firefighter, Blackbird, Water-hose, Hardhat, Rubber-hose and Fire-hose in English.
It is very difficult to classify the compound words as a single or multiple words. The (Durrani N., 2007) discussed three schemes of compound words in Urdu i.e. AB, A-o-B and A-e-B.

a. AB formation

This scheme involves only joining of two free morphemes e.g. مرہم پٹی (Bandaging) , میاں بیوی (husband wife), couple literally, حال احوال (condition). AB form of compounds is further classified into Dvanda, Tatpurusa, Karmadharaya and Divigu (Sabzwari S, 2002).

b. A-o-B formation

This formation of Urdu compounds contains a linking morpheme "o" and is represented by a character "و" , e.g.عجزوانکساری (soberness and humility), خط وکتابت (correspondence), امن وامان (law and order).

c. A-e-B formation

In this formation constituent words are connected with the help of one of the enclitic short morphemes; zer-e-izafat or hamza-e-izafat e.g. صدرمملکت (president) is combined by a diacritical mark "Zer" below ر called as zer-e-izafat while in جذبۂ دل (heart's spirit) and خلفائےاسلام (Islamic caliphs), the diacritical mark hamza (ء) is used as a hamza-e-izafat.
Some times the reduplication also produces ambiguity; whether it is treated as single or double word e.g. جگہ جگہ،آہستہ آہستہ،ساتھ ساتھ
(together, slowly, at every place)
Therefore there should be some rule for the identification of compound words. Thus these points should be considered while developing an Urdu stemmer.

4.5 Tokenization

The natural language processing applications need that the entered text should be tokenized for further processing. English language generally uses white spaces or punctuation marks for the identification of word boundaries.
Although in Urdu, space character is not present but with increasing usage of computer, it is now being used, for generating right shaping and to break up words.
Example: صدرنےدورسےوزیرکوآوازدی
(The President called away the Minister)
In the above sentence there are eight words (tokens) but computer will consider the whole sentence as a single word because the computer will generate tokens on the basis of space occurrence. As due to non-joiner characters (here ر،ے،و،ز) in the words, no space occurs among words, so this whole sentence is considered as a single word.
Therefore, during stemming, these non-joiner characters wrongly generate tokens of input text, stemmer will generate wrong resultantly stem.
Tokenization process should be error free, hence producing correct tokens before applying an Urdu stemmer.

4.6 Affixes Removal

The word affix is used by the linguists for expressing that where a bound morpheme precisely be joined to a word. The Prefix, Suffix and infix are called affixes. Due to the use of affixes, a single word may contain a lot of variants and by removing these affixes (prefix and suffix) from a word will result into a stem word e.g. بدگمانی (mis presumption). After removing the Urdu prefix and suffix from this word, produced a stem word گمان (presumption).

A lot of stemmers (except for Urdu) were developed for stripping off prefixes & suffixes from a word but there is little work done on infix stripping from a word. We cannot get stem word of an Urdu word by only stripping off prefixes and (or) suffixes e.g. اقوام (nations) , مساجد (mosques) , علوم (knowledge).

These words contain infixes and large amount of such type of words are present in Urdu. Special attention should be given to those Urdu words having infixes. After studying the morphology of Urdu words, it is noticed that if patterns for such type of words (having infixes) are made, then a correct stem could be achieved.

4.7 Exceptional Cases

a. Exceptional words

The removal of affixes (Prefixes and Suffixes) from a word produces a stem word but some times truncating these affixes leads to an erroneous stem e.g. نادار. Here نا is a prefix, where the stemmer eliminates it by producing دار , which is not a correct stem of the above stated word.

It means that in some words, the affixes play the role of stem characters and should not be removed. Such type of words should be treated as an exceptional case. In Urdu, there are a lot of words that can be treated as an exceptional case, thus for a stemmer, such word lists should be maintained in advance.

b. Urdu digits, Arithmetic Symbols and Punctuations

Urdu is read and written from right to left but when numbers are introduced, it is read and written from left to right.

حفصہ کی برتھ ڈے ۲فروری ۲۰۰۹ہے

(Hafsa's birthday is 2nd February 2009)

The Urdu digits (۰-۹), Arithmetic Symbols (+,-,*, /) and Punctuation marks (-,؟ , ، , ' , ',″ ,؛ ,:) should be treated as an exceptional case during developing Urdu stemmer.

4.8 Stem-word Dictionary

To check the accuracy of any stemmer, there should be a stem word dictionary. After studying relevant literature, it is noted that there is no stem dictionary available for Urdu text. Therefore, development of an Urdu stem dictionary is necessary for testing the accuracy of a stemmer on huge corpus.

4.9 Different Urdu words having same stem

In Urdu, there are a lot of words that are different in meaning but their stem is same e.g. تاثیر (characteristic) and آثار (signs). As we mentioned that the meaning of these two words are different from each other but their stem is same i.e. اثر Similarly the words ملوک (rulers) and ملایک (angels) are two different words having single script for their stem without diacritical marks i.e. ملک. The word ملک has two meanings i.e. ruler or angel. The word اصول (principles) and اصلیت (facts) have same stem i.e. اصل (principle/fact). Such type of words needs attention while developing a stemmer for Urdu language.

4.10 Code switching

Code switching, in linguistics, is the parallel use of more than one languages during conversation. The code switching in Urdu language is common and it accepts foreign words especially from English, e.g. ہے borrowed یہ کیمرہ (This Camera is borrowed).

In this example the Urdu text is from right to left-wards, while the English word "borrowed" is from left to right. The tokenization of the above sentence is performed in proper way electronically but Urdu stemmer will not stem the foreign word "borrowed", which is an issue.

5. Conclusion and Future Work

Stemmer is the core tool of any IR system. In this paper we have discussed some rule based English, Arabic, Persian and Urdu stemmers. Very less work has been done on Urdu stemmer due to its complex and rich morphology. Besides its own vocabulary, Urdu is also influenced by other morphology such as Arabic, Persian, Hindi, English etc. We have pointed out some challenges pertaining to the development of an Urdu stemmer. These issues should be considered while developing a rule based Urdu stemmer.

After studying different stemmers developed for Arabic, Persian and Urdu languages, we intend to develop an efficient rule based Urdu stemmer which will not only handle those Urdu words having prefixes and suffixes but also infixes. We will make patterns for handling infixes. For preprocessing of the proposed Urdu stemmer, Urdu stop word list will be maintained. An Urdu stem-word dictionary will also be prepared for evaluation purposes.

References

A. Mokhtaripour and S. Jahanpour, 2006. *Introduction to a New Farsi Stemmer*, CIKM'06, November 5–11, Arlington, Virginia, USA.

Durrani N. 2007. *Typology of Word and Automatic Word Segmentation in Urdu Text Corpus. National University of Computer and Emerging Sciences,*Lahore, Pakistan.

Eiman Tamah Al-Shammari, Jessica Lin, October 30, 2008. *Towards an Error-Free Arabic Stemming*, iNEWS'08, Napa Valley, California, USA.

Frakes, R.Baeza-Yates, 1992. *Information Retrieval: Data Structures & Algorithms*, New Jersey: Prentice Hall PTR.

J.B. Lovins, 1968. *Development of a stemming algorithm. Mechanical Translation and Computational Linguistics*, 11, pp.22–31.

Javed I. 1985. *New Urdu Grammar.* Advance Urdu Buru, New Dehali

Malik, M. G. Abbas. Boitet, Christian. Bhattcharyya, Pushpak. 2008. *Hindi Urdu Machine Transliteration using Finite-state Transducers*, proceedings of COLING 2008, Manchester, UK.

M.F. Porter, 1980. *An algorithm for suffix stripping*, Program, 14(3) pp. 130-137.

M Tashakori, MR Meybodi, F Oroumchian, 2003. *Bon: The Persian stemmer*, in Proc. 1st EurAsian Conf. on Information.

Payne, Thomas E. 2006. *Exploring Language Structure, A Student's Guide*. Cambridge: Cambridge University Press.

Q. Akram, A. Naseer and S. Hussain, 6-7 August 2009. *Assas-Band, an Affix- Exception-List Based Urdu Stemmer*, Proceedings of the 7th Workshop on Asian Language Resources, pp. 40–47, Suntec, Singapore.

Rizvi, S. & Hussain, M. 2005, *Analysis, Design and Implementation of Urdu Morphological Analyzer*, Engineering Sciences and Technology, SCONEST 2005. Student Conference, pp. 1-7

Sabzwari, S. 2002, *Urdu Quwaid.* Lahore: Sang-e-Meel Publication

S. Khoja and R. Garside, 1999. *Stemming Arabic Text,* Lancaster, UK, Computing Department, Lancaster University.

Sproat, R. 1992. *Morphology and Computation.* The MIT Press

Thabet, N. 2004. *Stemming the Qur'an* In the Proceedings of the Workshop on Computational Approaches to Arabic Script-based Languages.

Waqas A., Xuan W., Lu Li, Xiao-long W. 2006. A Survey of Automatic Urdu Language Processing. International Conference on Machine Learning and Cybernetics, pp: 4489-4494

Developing a New System for Arabic Morphological Analysis and Generation

Mourad Gridach
Mathematics and Computer Science Department Faculty of Science Dhar El Mehraz Fez
Mourad_i4@yahoo.fr

Noureddine Chenfour
Mathematics and Computer Science Department Faculty of Science Dhar El Mehraz Fez
chenfour@yahoo.fr

Abstract

Arabic morphology poses special challenges to computational natural language processing systems. Its rich morphology and the highly complex word formation process of roots and patterns make computational approaches to Arabic very challenging. In this paper we present an approach for morphological analysis and generation of Modern Standard Arabic (MSA). Our approach is based on Arabic morphological automaton technology. We take the special representation of Arabic morphology (root and scheme) to construct a set of morphological automaton which will be used directly in developing a system for Arabic morphological analysis and generation. Our approach for Arabic morphological analysis and generation can be used in different Arabic NLP applications such as Machine Translation (MT) and Information Retrieval (IR).

1 Introduction

Due to the rising importance of globalization and multilingualism, there is a need to build natural language processing (NLP) systems for an increasingly wider range of languages, including those languages that have traditionally not been the focus of NLP research. The development of NLP technologies for a new language is a challenging task since one needs to deal not only with language specific phenomena but also with a potential lack of available resources (e.g. lexicons, text, annotations).

Arabic is a language of rich morphology compared to other language especially European languages. It based on both derivational and inflectional morphology. The richness of Arabic morphology makes the analysis process difficult to deal. On the one hand, morphological analysis process is used in the most of the NLP applications such as information retrieval, spell-checking and machine translation. On the other hand, morphological analysis is the first step before syntactic analysis. Furthermore, it is an essential step in semantic analysis.

There has been much work on Arabic morphology. For an overview see (Al-Sughaiyer and Al-Kharashi, 2004). Generally speaking, morphological analysis of any word given consists of determining the values of a large number of features such as basic part-of-speech (i.e., noun, verb, etc.), gender, person, number, voice, information about the clitics, etc. (Habash, 2005). The most of the morphological analysis systems don't display the whole features of the word analyzed and some of them are destined for a special applications. We note that the morphological analysis systems available now have different aims, some of them have a commercial purpose and the other systems are available for research and evaluation (Attia, 2006).

In this paper we present an approach for Arabic morphological analysis and generation based on morphological automata and used a morphological database constructed using XMODEL (XML-base Morphological Definition Language). To develop an Arabic morphological automaton, we exploited particularities of Arabic morphology. The Arabic verbs and nouns are characterized by a special representation "root + scheme". Verbs and nouns are derived from roots by applying schemes to these roots to generate Arabic stems and then adding prefixes and suffixes to the stems to form a correct word in Arabic language. Table **1** show four schemes applied to the root "cml" (the work notion) (عمل) to generate four derived stems.

Scheme	facal	FAcil	fuccAl	Mafcal
Stem generated	عَمَل	عَامِل	عُمَّال	مَعْمَل
Transliteration	camal	CAmil	cummAl	macmal

Table 1 : Schemes generating stems from the root "cml" (عمل)

Proceedings of the 2nd Workshop on South and Southeast Asian Natural Language Processing (WSSANLP), IJCNLP 2011, , pages 52–57, Chiang Mai, Thailand, November 8, 2011.

2 Previous work

There has much been work on Arabic morphological analysis and generation. In this paragraph, we will present some of the most work referenced in the literature and well documented.

2.1 ElixirFM: an Arabic Morphological Analyzer by Otakar Smrz

ElixirFM is an online Arabic Morphological Analyzer for Modern Written Arabic developed by Otakar Smrz available for evaluation and well documented. This morphological analyzer is written in Haskell, while the interfaces in Perl. ElixirFM is inspired by the methodology of Functional Morphology (Forsberg & Ranta, 2004) and initially relied on the re-processed Buckwalter lexicon (Buckwalter, 2002). It contains two main components: a multi- purpose programming library and a linguistically morphological lexicon (Smrz, 2007). The advantage of this analyzer is that it gives to the user four different modes of operation (Resolve, Inflect, Derive and Lookup) for analyzing an Arabic word or text. But the system is limited coverage because it analyzes only words in the Modern Written Arabic.

2.2 MAGEAD: A Morphological Analyzer and Generator for Arabic Dialects

MAGEAD is one of the existing morphological analyzers for the Arabic language available for research. It's a functional morphology systems compared to Buckwalter morphological analyzer which models form-based morphology (M. Altantawy et al., 2010). To develop MAGEAD, they use a morphemic representation for all morphemes and explicitly define morphophonemic and orthographic rules to derive the allomorphs. The lexicon is developed by extending Elixir-FM's lexicon. The advantage of this analyzer is that it processes words from the morphology of the dialects which they considered as a novel work in this domain, but unfortunately this analyzer needs a complete lexicon for the dialects to make the evaluation more interesting and convincing, and to verify these claims.

2.3 Buckwalter Arabic Morphological Analyzer

This analyzer is considered as one of the most referenced in the literature, well documented and available for evaluation. It is also used by Linguistic Data Consortium (LDC) for POS tagging of Arabic texts, Penn Arabic Treebank, and the Prague Arabic Dependency Treebank (Atwell et al., 2004). It takes the stem as the base form and root information is provided. This analyzer contains over 77800 stem entries which represent 45000 lexical items. However, the number of lexical items and stems makes the lexicon voluminous and as result the process of analyzing an Arabic text becomes long.

2.4 Xerox Arabic Morphological Analysis and Generation

Xerox Arabic morphological Analyzer is well known in the literature and available for evaluation and well documented. This analyzer is constructed using Finite State Technology (FST) (Beesley, 1996; Beesley, 2000). It adopts the root and pattern approach. Besides this, it includes 4930 roots and 400 patterns, effectively generating 90000 stems. The advantages of this analyzer are, on the one hand, the ability of a large coverage. On the other hand, it is based on rules and also provides an English glossary for each word. But the system fails because of some problems such as the overgeneration in word derivation, production of words that do not exist in the traditional Arabic dictionaries (Darwish, 2002) and we can consider the volume of the lexicon as another disadvantage of this analyzer which could affect the analysis process.

3 Our approach

3.1 Lexicon

The lexicon of a language is the set of its valid lexical forms. As in any morphological analysis system, developing a high-quality lexicon is often the first step towards building a robust morphological analyzer, which is in turn the front-end to many NLP systems. There are two aspects that contribute to this enhancement level. The first aspect concerns the number of lexicon entries contained in the lexicon. Second aspect concerns the richness in linguistics information contained by the lexicon entries. BAMA lexicon is the best know in the literature and well documented. It used by large Arabic morphological analyzers (Elixir-FM and MAGEAD).For an overview of the existing Arabic lexicon see (Al-Sughaiyer and Al-Kharashi, 2004).

Nowadays, a new method was been implemented to represent, design and implement the lexicons. It is based on the Lexical Markup

Framework (LMF). LMF is the ISO-24613 standard for natural language processing (NLP) and lexicons. The US delegation is the first which started the work on LMF in 2003. In early 2004, the ISO/TC37 committee decided to form a common ISO project with Nicoletta Calzolari (Italy) as convenor and Gil Francopoulo (France) and Monte George (US) as editors. The aims of LMF are to provide a common model for the creation and use of lexical resources, to manage the exchange of data between and among these resources, and to enable the merging of large number of individual electronic resources to form extensive global electronic resources. This method for representing lexical resource covers all the natural languages. We note that for Arabic language, lexicons based on LMF are still in progress towards a standard for representing the Arabic linguistic resource.

Our approach for representing the lexicon is based on XMODEL (XML-based Morphological Definition Language). In this approach, the Arabic lexicon contains morphological classes, morphological properties and morphological rules. Morphological classes allow gathering a set of morphological components having the same nature, the same morphological characteristics and the same semantic actions. For the morphological properties, they allow characterizing the different morphological components represented by the morphological classes; they contain morphological descriptors (the features) that would be assigned to different morphological components (the property "Gender" distinguishes between masculine and feminine components). Finally, morphological rules allow combining the morphological components to generate correct language words. They are considered as a generator of language words. We note that until now, our morphological database contains 5970 entries. The use of XMODEL allows representing the morphological database independent of processing which will be applied and allows a considerable reduction of morphological entries.

3.2 System description

In this part we describe the Arabic morphological analyzer. So as to develop this analyzer, first of all, we developed an Arabic morphological database using XMODEL language integrating all the entries suitable for Arabic language. Then, we generated a set of Arabic morphological automata representing a specific morphological category. Finally, a framework is developed to handle the lexicon and the morphological automata.

The presented work involves five steps. In this paragraph, we provide a brief description of the principles of this work. As input, the proposed technique accepts an Arabic text. The first step is to apply a tokenization process to the text given. Then, a set of AMAUT (Arabic Morphological AUTomata) are loaded, in a second step. The part-of-speech is determined in the third step. After that, the method determines all possible affixes. Then the next step consists of extracting the morpho-syntactic features according to the valid affixes.

The tokenization process consists of extracting all the words from the text given. A set of Arabic morphological automata are loaded from a package that contains all the implemented Arabic morphological automata. Then, the approach determines which AMAUT is suitable for that word. The result may be one or more AMAUT loaded. We note that the size of the final AMAUT generated is about 120 MB. Then, the method determines the part-of-speech. If the word analyzed is a noun or a verb, the method determines if it contains a scheme. Then, if it is a verb, the method determines the type of the verb (strong, weak, or incomplete), its tense ("mADI" /ماضي/, "muDAric" /مضارع/ or "eamr" /أمر/), its voice (active or passive), etc. If it is a noun, we determine if it is a derived noun or particular noun. If it is a particle, the method determines if it is a preposition particle /حروف الجر/, conjunction particle /حروف العطف /, etc. After that, the method applied a process of extracting the possible affixes attached to the word analyzed. The next step consists of extracting the morpho-syntactic features according to the valid affixes and the scheme. Additional information is extracted called in our approach morphological descriptors. They describe the word analyzed and they are very useful especially in Natural Language Processing applications. Finally, the morphological analyzer displays the results in a table where each row contains the word analyzed and all the data characterizing this word (see Figure 1).

Generally speaking, morpho-syntactic features displayed by the morphological analyzer are very rich regarding the information given. It concerns the morphological level; the syntactic and semantic level which makes the richness of our system compared to the others system. The utility of this richness comes especially when the system will be used in NLP applications. Here are the most important features given by the system.

- The word gender: masculine or feminine.
- The word person: first, second or third person.
- The word number: singular, dual or plural.
- The word case: "marfUc" (مرفوع), "manSUb" (منصوب), "majrUr" (مجرور), "majzUm" (مجزوم).
- The type of the word: verb, noun or particle.
- If the word is a verb, we give its tense: present ("ealmuDAric": المضارع), past ("ealmADI": الماضي) or imperative ("ealeamr": الأمر). We also give its voice: active or passive.
- The scheme of the word is given if available.

Figure **1** shows the morphological analysis results of some words analyzed using the presented morphological analyzer. The displays the Part-of-speech (verb, noun or particle), the original scheme is displayed in column B because Arabic has this particularity which is summarized in that some words might be conjugated forms of other words like "afcalu", "afcilu ", "afculu", these three words are all conjugated forms of "facala". The gender (masculine or feminine) is displayed in column D, the person (first, second or third person) is displayed in column E, the number (singular, dual or plural) is displayed in column F. For the column G, it concerns some properties that characterize the word analyzed and they are very useful to the user. Some morphological descriptors are displayed in column H. Finally, the column I and J show the affixes attached to the word.

Lexical Table of File : arab files\dfa01.txt

A	B	C	D	E	F	G	H	I	J
Morphological	Original Scheme	Scheme	Gender	Person	Number	Properties	Morphological Descriptors	Prefixes	Suffixes
yatadaHrajAni	[tafacala],	□	GMa	,Fr3	,NDI	Strong Verb,MOD,ACT,	Raf,	[y]	[Ani]
eaSTaffa	[eifcalla],	□	GFe,GMa	,Fr1	,NSg	Strong Verb,ACT,MOD,	Def,NaS	[e]	[a]
eaSTaffa	[eifcalla],	□	GFe,GMa	,Fr1	,NSg	Strong Verb,ACT,MOD,	Def,NaS	[e]	[a]
eaSTaffu	[eifcalla],	□	GFe,GMa	,Fr1	,NSg	Strong Verb,ACT,MOD,	Def,Raf,	[e]	[u]
yacuddu	[cadda],	□	GMa	,Fr3	,NSg	Incomplete Verb,MOD,	Def,Raf,	[y]	[u]
yacidu	[wacala, wacila, wacula],	□	GMa	,Fr3	,NSg	Weak Verb,ACT,MOD,	Def,Raf,	[y]	[u]
yucda	[facA, faciya],	□	GMa	,Fr3	,NSg	Weak Verb,PAS,MOD,	NaS,Jaz,	[y]	[a]
yari~a	[wacala, wacila, wacula],	□	GMa	,Fr3	,NSg	Weak Verb,ACT,MOD,	Def,NaS	[y]	[a]
yar~i	[eafcA],	□	GMa	,Fr3	,NSg	Weak Verb,ACT,MOD,	NaS,Jaz,	[y]	[i]
yur~a	[facA, faciya],	□	GMa	,Fr3	,NSg	Weak Verb,PAS,MOD,	NaS,Jaz,	[y]	[a]
yari~u	[wacala, wacila, wacula],	□	GMa	,Fr3	,NSg	Weak Verb,ACT,MOD,	Def,Raf,	[y]	[u]

Figure 1: A morphological analysis of some Arabic words using the presented system

It should be noted that the presented system could be used in both analysis and generation unlike some Arabic morphological analyzers which cannot be converted to generators in a straightforward manner (Cavalli-Sforza, 2000; Buckwalter, 2004; Habash, 2004 ;).

4 Evaluation

To evaluate our system, we select two of the best known morphological analyzers in the literature: ElixirFM by Otakar Smrž (Otakar Smrž and Viktor Bielický, 2010) and Xerox Arabic Morphological Analyzer. We note that the corpus used for the evaluation is taken from a standard input text provided by ALECSO (Arab League, Educational, Cultural and Scientific Organization) which organized a competition in April 2009 of the Arabic Morphological Analyzers in Damascus.

The evaluation process shows that our morphological analyzer is strong concerning the features given by each analyzer which makes our system useful for the most of NLP applications unlike the others; they are destined for specific applications. In addition, the presented morphological analyzer gives more additional information about each word analyzed and more precision.

In the evaluation done we process words in a corpus selected from ALECSO input text containing different part-of-speech (verbs, nouns and particles), then, we calculate accuracy of each analyzer as: S = number of words with good solutions / number of words. Table 2 provides the evaluation results of the three analyzers. Note that Table 2 contains in each column of the analyzers the number of words (nouns, verbs and particles) with no solution.

POS	The number	Xerox Morphological Analyzer	ElixirFM	Our System
Nouns	576	60	56	40
Verbs	457	31	24	19
Particles	167	42	45	-
Total	1200	133	125	59
Accuracy (%)		88.91%	89.58%	95.08%

Table 2: The evaluation process results

The analyzer presented in this paper reaches an accuracy of 95.08% which will make it one of the best existing morphological analyzers for Arabic language and it will be very useful for the next future works to be done in NLP applications such as syntactic and semantic analysis, machine translation, information retrieval, etc.

5 Conclusion

In this paper, we have discussed some previous work in this area of research which is the most referenced in the literature. Then, we have outlined some challenges of computational Arabic morphology. After that, we presented an approach to develop a morphological analyzer and generator for Arabic language. To develop this system for Arabic morphological analysis, the need to develop a lexicon is an essential stage. So, we used a new language for representing, designing and implementing the linguistic resource. It is based on a reduced XML lexicon and it can be used not only in morphological level, but in the other levels such as syntactic and semantic level. Finally, our approach could be used in NLP applications such as machine translation and information retrieval.

Appendix (1): Letter mappings

ا	:	A	س	:	S	ك	:	k
ب	:	B	ش	:	^	ل	:	l
ت	:	T	ص	:	S	م	:	m
ث	:	~	ض	:	D	ن	:	n
ج	:	J	ط	:	T	هـ	:	h
ح	:	H	ظ	:	Z	و	:	w
خ	:	X	ع	:	c	ي	:	y
د	:	D	غ	:	g	ى	:	A
ذ	:	V	ف	:	f	ة	:	t
ر	:	R	ق	:	q	ء	:	e
ز	:	Z						

References

Al-Sughaiyer Imad A. and Al-Kharashi Ibrahim A. 2004. Arabic morphological analysis techniques: A comprehensive survey. Journal of the American Society for Information Science and Technology, 55(3):189–213

Altantawy Mohamed, Nizar Habash, Owen Rambow, and Ibrahim Saleh. 2010. Morphological Analysis and Generation of Arabic Nouns: A Morphemic Functional Approach. In Proceedings of the Language Resource and Evaluation Conference (LREC-2010), Malta.

Attia, M. 2006. An Ambiguity-Controlled Morphological Analyzer for Modern Standard Arabic Modelling Finite State Networks. The Challenge of Arabic for NLP/MT Conference, the British Computer Society, London.

Atwell E., Al-Sulaiti L., Al-Osaimi S., Abu Shawar B.. 2004. A Review of Arabic Corpus Analysis Tools, JEP-TALN 04, Arabic Language Processing, Fès, 19-22 April.

Beesley KR 1996. Arabic Finite-State Morphological Analysis and Generation, Proceedings of the 16th conference on Computational linguistics, Vol 1. Copenhagen, Denmark: Association for Computational Linguistics, pp 89-94.

Beesley KR. 2000. Finite-State Non-Concatenative Morphotactics SIGPHON-2000, Proceedings of the Fifth Workshop of the ACL Special Interest Group in Computational Phonology, p. 1-12, August 6, 2000, Luxembourg.

Buckwalter T. 2002. Buckwalter Arabic Morphological Analyzer Version 1.0. Linguistic Data Consortium, University of Pennsylvania, LDC Catalog No.: LDC2002L49.

Buckwalter, T. 2004. Buckwalter Arabic Morphological Analyzer Version 2.0. Linguistic Data Consortium, catalog number LDC2004L02 and ISBN 1-58563-324-0.

Cavalli-Sforza, V., Soudi. A, and Teruko M. 2000. Arabic Morphology Generation Using a Concatenative Strategy. In Proceedings of the 1st Conference of the North American Chapter of the Association for Computational Linguistics (NAACL 2000), Seattle, USA.

Darwish K. (2002). Building a Shallow Morphological Analyzer in One Day, Proceedings of the workshop on Computational Approaches to Semitic Languages in the 40th Annual Meeting of the Association for Computational Linguistics (ACL-02). Philadelphia, PA, USA.

Habash Nizar. 2004. Large scale lexeme based Arabic orphological generation. In Proceedings of Traitement Automatique du Langage Naturel (TALN-04). Fez, Morocco.

Habash Nizar and Rambow Owen. 2005. Arabic Tokenization, Part-of-Speech Tagging and Morphological Disambiguation in One Fell Swoop. In Proceedings of the 43rd Annual Meeting of the Association for Computational Linguistics ACL, pages 573–580, Ann Arbor.

Forsberg M. and Ranta A. 2004. Functional Morphology ICFP'04, Proceedings of the Ninth ACM SIGPLAN International Conference of Functional Programming, September 19-21, Snowbird, Utah

Ibrahim, K. 2002. Al-Murshid fi Qawa'id Al-Nahw wa Al-Sarf [The Guide in Syntax and Morphology Rules]. Amman, Jordan, Al-Ahliyyah for Publishing and Distribution.

Otakar Smrz (2007). ElixirFM. Implementation of Functional Arabic Morphology. In ACL Proceedings of the Workshop on Computational Approaches to Semitic Languages: Common Issues and Resources, pages 1–8, Prague, Czech Republic.

Otakar Smrž and Viktor Bielický. 2010. ElixirFM. Functional Arabic Morphology, http://sourceforge.net/projects/elixir-fm/.

Author Index